Generation WTF

GENERATION

WTF

From "What the #%$&?" to a Wise, Tenacious, and Fearless You

Advice from Experts and WTFers Just Like You

Christine B. Whelan, PhD

TEMPLETON PRESS

Templeton Press
300 Conshohocken State Road, Suite 550
West Conshohocken, PA 19428
www.templetonpress.org

Designed and typeset by Gopa and Ted2, Inc.

In some cases, names have been changed at the request of the subjects quoted in the book.

The Self-Control Scale used in part in chapter 4 is reprinted with permission from Elsevier. From Rosenbaum, M. "A schedule for Assessing Self-Control Behaviors: Preliminary Findings," *Behavior Therapy*, 11(1), 13.

The Procrastination Scale used in part in chapter 5 is reprinted with permission from Elsevier. From Lay, C. (1986). "At Last, My Research Article on Procrastination," *Journal of Research in Personality*, 20(4), 22.

The Materialism Scale used in chapter 6 is reprinted with permission from the University of Chicago Press. From Richins, M. L., & Dawson, S. (1992). "A Consumer Values Orientation for Materialism and Its Measurement: Scale Development and Validation," *Journal of Consumer Research*, 19(3), 303-316.

The Narcissistic Personality Inventory, copyright © 1988 by the American Psychological Association used in chapter 8, adapted with permission. Raskin, R., & Terry, H. (1988). "A principal-components analysis of the Narcissistic Personality Inventory and further evidence of its construct validity," *Journal of Personality and Social Psychology*, 54(5), 890-902.

Library of Congress Cataloging-in-Publication Data

Whelan, Christine B., 1977-
  Generation WTF / Christine B. Whelan.
    p. cm.
  Includes bibliographical references.
  ISBN-13: 978-1-59947-347-5 (pbk. : alk. paper)
  ISBN-10: 1-59947-347-X (pbk. : alk. paper) 1. Young adults—Psychology.
2. Young adults—Life skills guides. 3. Self-realization. 4. Success. I. Title.
  HQ799.5W54 2010
  646.700842—dc22

2010030875

Printed in the United States of America

11 12 13 14 15 16   10 9 8 7 6 5 4 3 2 1

Contents

PART III: GET FEARLESS

Introduction

I WAS ON TRACK, OR AT LEAST I THOUGHT I WAS. I DID WELL IN SCHOOL.
YEAH, I WAS IN SOME DEBT, BUT EVERYONE ELSE WAS, TOO.
I WAS PLANNING ON A GOOD JOB OUT OF COLLEGE TO PAY IT ALL BACK,
ANYWAY. BUT THEN, IN THE LAST YEAR OR SO, EVERYTHING CHANGED.
WHERE ARE THE JOBS? WHERE ARE ALL THE OPPORTUNITIES THAT
OUR GENERATION THOUGHT WE'D HAVE? IT WAS LIKE, WTF.
I MEAN, WHAT JUST HAPPENED HERE? THE RUG JUST GOT PULLED
OUT FROM UNDER US AND SUDDENLY YOU WANT US TO BECOME
THESE RESILIENT, FRUGAL PEOPLE? HOW? —ADAM

If you're in your twenties trying to excel in a world that doesn't seem to be working the way you'd hoped, then you're part of "Generation WTF"—savvy, but frustrated, young adults who are asking:

▶ What happened to the promises of a bright future?
▶ What happened to the jobs?
▶ And what do we do now that the rules have changed?

Until recently, the vast majority of Generation WTF thought they'd earn $75,000 a year by thirty. Now, fewer than half of you think you'll be financially better off than your parents someday. Gone are the dreams of big-ticket jobs: The median income for young adults is

Are You a Member of Generation WTF?

- ▶ I'm 18–25 years old.

- ▶ I'm optimistic but unsure of how exactly to achieve my goals.

- ▶ I want to have more control over my life.

- ▶ I'm willing to work hard, but I'm not sure where to focus my energy.

- ▶ I could use some practical information about personal finance.

- ▶ I'm looking for research-based suggestions—and not to be told what to do.

about $27,000—for those fortunate enough to find work at all. After being raised to believe that fame and fortune were around the corner, suddenly the road has more twists and turns than you expected.

We all know what "WTF" usually stands for: It's an exclamation of frustration and anger. It's a protest in the face of defeat—What happened? Why did things get so messed up?—and it's an understandable reaction to a recession that has hit young adults harder than any other group.

But if you're like most of Generation WTF, despite the bleak headlines, you're still optimistic. So rather than focusing on the frustration and protest that WTF usually stands for, it's time to reclaim the acronym as a battle cry for a positive future: Generation WTF will be a **W**ise, **T**enacious, and **F**earless generation, strengthened by purpose and hope.

This book is your guide to moving from frustration and protest to a wise, tenacious, and fearless you.

In this book you'll:

Get Wise

▶ Figure out what drives you—and where you want to go.

▶ Uncover the purpose and meaning behind your choices.

▶ Get honest about your feelings.

Get Tenacious

▶ Set SMARTER goals.

▶ Determine the tricks that work for you as you set a path to achieve those goals.

▶ Find out how it's possible to break out of the procrastination-stress cycle.

Get Fearless

▶ Be empowered to make smart choices about money.

▶ Learn how to avoid arguments and ace interviews.

▶ Begin thinking outside the "you" box to strengthen relationships with family, friends, and community.

What *Happened*? And Where Did All the Jobs Go?

For two decades, Americans believed the only direction was up: Housing prices rose, the stock market climbed ever higher, and individual spending soared. Materialism beat out thrift, instant gratification was cooler than self-control, and the runaway self-help bestseller of 2006, *The Secret*, told us that all we had to do was think about success hard enough, and it would magically find its way to us.

Then, in the fall of 2008, the zeitgeist changed: The stock market plummeted, jobless rates rose—and the era of seemingly never-ending prosperity came to a screeching halt. Restaurants replaced their $150 tasting menus with $30 prix fixe options, companies "downsized," eliminating jobs in nearly every sector of the economy, and families canceled holiday travel plans as they searched for fun on a limited budget. By the end of the year, some 60 percent of Americans reported they were "struggling," according to the Gallup well being index. Time didn't heal all wounds: 2009 and 2010 weren't much better with unemployment topping 10 percent and disillusionment about the aftereffects of costly corporate bailouts.

And this bad news hit your generation particularly hard. For some, there was a panic about how to afford the skyrocketing cost of college. Others were overwhelmed by a sinking feeling about the bleak job prospects on the other side. The average college graduate will leave school with more than $20,000 in school loans, and upwards of $4,000 in credit card debt, a figure that's spiked some 40 percent since 2005. And jobs to pay off these debts are harder to come by: In May 2009, as college seniors graduated, one national study found that only 20 percent of students who had applied for a job actually had one. By 2010 the job market was picking up a bit, but still only about a quarter of seniors who wanted jobs landed gigs by graduation day.

Even if the economy improves dramatically in the coming years— which we all hope it does—Generation WTF has been shaken up. Many of you feel pissed off, and understandably so. But all hope is not lost: In your hands right now are some powerful strategies for long-term success.

The Experiment That Could Change Your Life

This is no ordinary self-help book, because I'm no ordinary self-help book writer. I'm a young sociology professor, and I wrote my doctoral dissertation on the self-help industry. In the decade or so since college, I have studied who buys self-help books, what advice is popular and why. I have crafted rigorous content analyses of bestselling titles to uncover the "formula" of their successes. I catalogued the advice of hundreds of guides to find the ones that had real research (and the ones that were mostly made-up garbage). I've explored the assumptions, sociology, and psychology of personal improvement. And along the way, I've combed through the advice to find the nuggets of enduring wisdom in these popular paperbacks.

The advice in this book comes from three sources: bestselling, timeless self-help books, psychology experiments about behavior change, and real-life experiences of Generation WTFers just like you. In January 2009 some eighty students enrolled in my class on self-help books in modern society. The goal of the course was simple: Students read a few of the bestselling (and best) advice books from the last 150 years and applied them in their own lives. They wrote weekly journal entries on how the advice was working (and not working) on a personal level—and suggested techniques and tips for how to adapt the advice to be most useful for Generation WTF. In 2010 I tested more advice with a different group of students in a class on social change. And along the way I kept in touch with many of these young adults as they graduated and entered "the real world."

The book you are holding in your hand is the product of all the advice books I've analyzed—and the road-tested experiences of Generation WTFers like you. While some names have been changed, the quotes in this book are from real WTF testers and used with their permission. Wherever possible, they are unedited to give you the most accurate version of their experiences. Think of this as a condensed guide to the best advice out there—specifically tailored to focus on the concerns of your generation.

In the 2009 test I chose seven core books and sections from dozens more guides, nearly all of which spent weeks—if not years—on bestseller lists and have been highly ranked and lauded by mental health, business, or financial professionals. My testers read *Self-Help* by Samuel Smiles (1859) and *The Road Less Traveled* by M. Scott Peck (1978) for advice on stick-to-itiveness. They weighed advice from *Thrift* by Samuel Smiles (1876), Suze Orman's *The 9 Steps to Financial Freedom* (1997), and *The Finish Rich Workbook* by David Bach (2003) for advice on budgeting and personal finance. For relationships with friends, significant others, and colleagues, they read *How to Win Friends and Influence People* by Dale Carnegie (1937), and for future planning they took *The 7 Habits of Highly Effective People* by Stephen Covey (1987) for a spin. In the 2010 test, I asked a different group of students to read a new book, *59 Seconds: Think a Little, Change a Lot* (2009), by respected psychologist and social critic Richard Wiseman.

And while the best nuggets of self-help advice in these books made a real impact on their lives, the Generation WTF testers told me they wanted to know *why*. Sure, nice stories could be inspiring, but was there any research on the *why* and *how* of breaking bad habits and making positive changes? "I really don't like being told what to do without some

Generation WTF on Old-School Self-Help

- ► 95 percent of testers said the advice offered was **valuable to their lives**.

- ► 86 percent of testers agreed that they had **learned some new information**.

- ► 92 percent reported that they had **learned something new about *themselves***.

- ► 86 percent of testers reported that advice **reminded them of skills they'd forgotten**.

proof," said Kim. "I want to see the research. Does the advice work in reality, or just in some ideal universe?"

These were excellent questions—and ones that guided me as I wrote this book.

Carnegie, Covey, and other bestselling advice authors studied the work of ancient philosophers and thinkers to craft their now-classic guides. But in the last few decades psychologists and behavioral economists have taken things a step further: They've tested out what advice works—and why.

The advice in this book has been tested—and proved worthy—in a number of ways:

- ► It's got real research to back it up;
- ► It's been tested by your peers;
- ► It's based on some long-respected (if forgotten) advice that's been personalized for your generation.

Self-help earned its reputation as a frivolous genre after decades of quick-fix solutions and meaningless platitudes. But advice literature didn't used to be so vapid. Indeed, historically the message of self-help advises individuals to build their character through virtuous behavior, build a career through hard work and delayed gratification, build relationships through commitment, and build a nest egg through thrift.

@Exclusive Bonus Features Online!

Go to **www.generationwtf.com** to check out a special bonus chapter: "Why Most Self-Help Books Suck (and Why This One Is Different)." Learn the tricks of the self-help trade, how to be a savvy consumer, and how to take control of your own reading experience.

PLUS:

▶ Personality tests and psychological inventories to help you get honest about who you are

▶ Ways to connect with others on the same path

▶ WTF-specific planners and other tools to get you started on your goals

▶ And lots more—available only to those wise, tenacious, and fearless enough to join the Generation WTF community

You're a no-BS generation. You tell it like it is and aren't afraid to challenge authority. You want honest advice, not inner-child soul-searching or corner-cutting business tricks. But you don't have to come up with these axioms on your own. By turning back to some of the most useful advice offered by bestselling self-help books of the last 150 years, you can revive the virtues that will carry you through today's crises. In short, you need yesterday's self-help today.

How to Read This Book

This book will give you examples, exercises, and real-world guidance for how to successfully navigate school, work, and personal life in your twenties. It's geared toward college seniors and young adults just entering the job market—and its advice has been road-tested by members of your generation.

Based on my extensive academic research on self-help books and the experiences of young adults like you, this book will highlight the best advice from retro gurus and put a modern spin on it. My job as a self-help scholar, professor, and advice-giver is to present these ancient truths in a new form—one specifically crafted for Generation WTF as you head into an uncertain workforce. The rug has been pulled out from under you in many ways, but redefining that exclamation of angst into one of hope is within your reach.

While the speed-readers among you could probably knock it out in a day, the point isn't to get through this book in a certain period of time. *Generation WTF* is an action manual full of tips, techniques, and exercises that will only make a difference in your life it you actually *do* them. So take your time. Challenge yourself to make commitments and personalize the suggestions. Get out a pen, pencil, or go online. Repeated studies show that just reading or thinking about personal change isn't nearly as effective as writing down goals and trying things out in your own life.

Learning the skills you need to thrive ain't a cake-walk, which is why this is a book, not a pamphlet. I've consciously divided the advice into three big steps that build on each other. The first two steps are focused inward, on you, and the last step is devoted to taking that character growth and personal understanding into the big wide world. Think of it this way: If you want to have a meaningful career, you have to learn some skills first. If you want to have loving relationships, you've got to be clear on who you are. This book is built on those same principles.

To get the most benefit, you might consider reading one section over the course of a week and then testing out the advice for another week or two before going on to the next section. There's no prize for finishing fastest, and there's no one who will force you to be thoughtful about the exercises. (Welcome to the joys of adulthood.) But my research about behavior change tells me that since you are reading this book, you've got what it takes to become wise, tenacious, and fearless.

In the first section, you'll get *Wise*—and learn about yourself. You'll fill out surveys to uncover your strengths and growth areas and learn dozens of strategies to keep you focused on honest self-reflection throughout the book. Then, with lots of interactive exercises, you'll figure out your values and lay out a personal mission statement that will guide you as you become *Tenacious* by setting—and achieving—goals. Finally, in the last section, you'll get *Fearless* about your finances and interpersonal relationships. By combining these three elements of your personality—your inner wisdom, the tenacity to achieve your goals, and a fearless understanding of how to use money wisely and get involved in your community—you're off to a great start for an empowered future. It's all ahead, so let's get started for a wise, tenacious, and fearless you!

part i

GET WISE

chapter 1

Who Are You?

Why Understanding Your Values Is the First Step to Success

HOW DO I FIND MY PATH AND DIRECTION IN LIFE? HOW DO I KNOW WHAT I WANT TO BECOME OR WHAT I'M DESTINED TO BE? —*EVAN*

For most of your life, you've been told what to do. But now, "real life" is beginning—and it's your turn to call the shots. What do you want to do? Who do you want to be? This chapter is about asking some deep questions about yourself and finding your purpose in the world. To achieve that, this chapter will challenge you to

- Figure out your values,
- Vocalize your purpose, and
- Create a personal mission statement to guide you on the path to a wise, tenacious, and fearless you.

Are you ready to jump right in?

It's 2021 and, tragically, you've died young. You're watching your own memorial service where your friends, family members, coworkers, and members of your groups or clubs are going to speak about who you were. What do you want them to say? What did you do with your life?

Brutal, right? But let it play out, because it's one of the best ways to figure out what you value in life . . . while you've still got decades to make it happen. Take some time with this question. Daydream realistically about where you see yourself. Are you a parent? A community leader? Who is most central in your life? Do you want your friends to describe you as loyal? Hardworking? Optimistic? And are you on track to make this happen?

This powerful exercise is used by several self-help books, including Stephen Covey's *The 7 Habits of Highly Effective People* and David Bach's *The Finish Rich Workbook*. The point is to demonstrate that being busy and getting a lot done aren't the same as accomplishing your goals. This is a crucial message as you struggle with the purpose, direction, and meaning of your life.

"Imagining my own funeral in all its intricacies was a very intense experience that provided a very good mental image of who I want to grow to be," said Chris. "Once I began thinking about how I wanted to be remembered by those that know me, I really started thinking about what type of person I am and what type of person I want to strive to be. Though at times I fall short of this ideal, this habit has increased my awareness of my own actions in relation to who I want to be."

Fellow tester Carly said she'd had a too-personal experience with this scenario recently when a close friend died in a car accident. That tragedy, and this exercise, reminded her of what was really important in life. "I think that people need to do what they want to be remembered by. Whether it's a first impression or a last, think about the end result of the behavior you are exhibiting. It also leads to goals in life. When I think about the end of my life, I have a picture of where I want to be. Having the end in mind keeps me focused on the goals I hope to achieve."

You might think this is a really morbid way to begin an optimistic book—but don't skip over this exercise. By thinking about who you want to be and what you want to accomplish now, in your twenties, you are much better prepared to achieve those goals in the coming years. In previous generations, self-help was mostly for people in their forties and fifties who were realizing, belatedly, that they wanted something different from their lives. Fortunately, you can start a lot sooner.

In 2021, I will be _____ years old. I will have accomplished the following things:

1. _____

2. _____

3. _____

4. _____

What are the phrases that you'd hope to hear as those closest to you describe your personality and your core values?

1. _____

2. _____

3. _____

4. _____

Take a moment to consider: Are you living your life now so that people would say this about you . . . if you died tomorrow? If you are at all uncertain, it's time to focus on living your values.

What Are Values?

Your values guide your decisions, both big and small. Values are what's important to you, what you cherish about yourself and your relationships with others. Values are about who you want to be—and yet, for some reason, we spend very little time thinking about our values.

In his bestselling financial planning guide, *The Finish Rich Workbook*, David Bach tells readers that knowing their values—and getting clear about who they want to be—is the first step toward achieving financial goals. "When you understand what's important to you, it becomes much easier to focus on who you want to *be*, then on what you want to *do*, and, finally, on what 'stuff' you *really* want to have," he writes. But knowing your values helps a lot more than just your financial life: Having a clear sense of who you want to be will guide every one of your life decisions—for the better.

Values are different than goals, he warns: Goals are what you want to do, while values are who you want to be. Having a million dollars is a goal, not a value. Becoming famous is a goal, not a value. But to accomplish either of those goals means understanding what's important to you as an individual.

In his Value Circle™ exercise, Bach asks readers to list the five core values by which they live (or want to live) their lives. Security, health, strong marriage, family, and fun might pop up on a Value Circle™. Or perhaps freedom, happiness, peace of mind, spirituality, and balance.

Knowing your values stops the vicious cycle of working hard at unsatisfying jobs only to go into credit card debt for things to dull the pain, explains Bach. "Trust me, the Value Circle™ exercise can change your life." And after watching dozens of WTF testers try this exercise, it seems Bach is right.

Try it for yourself: What are your values?

1. _____

2. _____

3. _____

4. _____

5. _____

Having problems narrowing it down? Erin started with a list of twenty-eight and cut it down to ten but then she was stuck: Her top ten values were security, happiness, fun, family, marriage, making a difference, fulfillment, balance, education, and kindness. To narrow the list down to six, she focused on the life she wanted to live today—not in the future—and dropped security, family, marriage, and fulfillment.

"Those are values that I want to work toward being able to have in the future but are not at the top of my values list in my twenty-two-year-old college life." She combined the ideas of kindness and the desire to make a difference into one value, generosity, and had her five core values: happiness, balance, fun, education, and generosity.

How to Live Your Values

For many Generation WTFers, the Value Circle™ exercise was challenging because it exposed a disconnect between their cherished ideas of themselves and the way they were actually living their lives. If you feel the same way, these WTF tips will help you close the gap:

Generation WTF Gets Values

▶ **As you think about your values, you might be surprised what you find.** Jon had thought that his goal was to make a lot of money—but after thinking through his values, he realized that it was freedom that he wanted, less so than a specific amount of cash in a bank account.

▶ **Write it down.** "I had never really outlined my values. I had thought about them before, but actually writing them down made it easier for me to remember," said Tim.

▶ **Live your values.** "I am very proud of my Value Circle™," reported Victoria, of her five chosen values of health, knowledge, relationships, happiness, and faith. "I think it may operate in an almost self-fulfilling prophecy way," she mused: Just by listing certain values, she felt more likely to act in a way that would fulfill them. Perhaps because of this, Victoria said she believed she had "greatly benefited from examining my life and really pinpointing values that are important to me."

1. Think about Your Values—and Write Them Down

Kim said her core values included family, love, security, friendship, and independence, and found the charts and exercises in *The Finish Rich Workbook* "extremely helpful" because "writing my goals down did in fact make me feel more obligated and motivated to complete them."

We'll see this time and again with behavioral change advice: Actually writing things down really makes a difference. Because writing is a powerful way to tell your story, sort your thoughts, and commit yourself to change, you'll do a lot of writing in this book. Keep a pencil or pen, and a journal, handy.

2. *It's OK to Write in Pencil, Not Pen*

Jaye said the Value Circle™ helped her focus on the purpose of her education—not just having fun and learning—but working toward a fulfilling career. Still, she was sensitive to the fact that her chosen values might change over time. "As life changes, this circle will change and I could probably do the same exercise in a month and could potentially get very different answers, but I suppose that is why [Bach] recommends completing the exercises in pencil instead of pen," she concluded.

3. *Put That List Front and Center*

Just making the list wasn't going to do much to change their day-to-day behaviors, testers realized. One wrote out her values on the back of a business card and stuck it in the clear-plastic window of her wallet. Every time she opened her wallet, she'd see her list of values.

Molly taped her Value Circle™—with independence topping the charts—on the mirror above her dresser, "so that I can see it every day. It reminds me that if I want to live independently I need to save an extra few dollars a day, so I can pay for the apartment to live in after college or be adventurous and go to a new country. Those values should always be on the top of my priority list, every single day." And while Molly recognized she was young and just starting out, "I now know that I need to start prioritizing my life according to my values starting now and not when it is too late. Understanding and having written

---

**Most Common Entries
in Generation WTF Value Circles:**

► Family	► Health	► Strong marriage	► Independence
► Security	► Career	► Love	► Friendship
► Fun	► Education	► Happiness	► Excitement

---

down the important aspects of my life has motivated me to start being independent now. I plan on finding a job at school my senior year so I can save up the money to have my own place after I graduate. It is something that has always been important to me. I now know that I need to start acting like it is important to me, not just thinking it."

Is Your Internal GPS Leading You in the Right Direction?

Once you've listed your five core values, it's time to take a good, hard look at yourself and ask, "Am I following those values as best as I can in my everyday life?" Or, put another way, would you expect your friends, family members, and colleagues to use those five phrases in their descriptions of you at your funeral? If not, it might be time to recalibrate your internal GPS and make sure you're headed on the right track.

In *The Road Less Traveled*, M. Scott Peck argues that our view of reality is like a map—and if that map is wrong, we'll get lost and make poor choices. To make sure you're on the right path, you've got to face the truth, find your real map, and live life accordingly. By avoiding challenge, we avoid the truth. By ignoring our values, we're headed in the wrong direction.

Josh said it was very useful to think about his decisions as directional choices on a map of life. "This exercise really helped show me that I can make subtle changes in my life that have a big impact. In order to be responsible for myself, I have to be true to myself. In order to be true to myself, I need to be patient and able to reflect on the situation, so all these areas tie in together."

If your internal GPS is on the fritz, you'll feel like you are working hard, but not accomplishing your goals. It's as if you're lost in some suburban subdivision from hell, making turns blindly, going in circles endlessly. Without the right map—without the right values and a clear sense of purpose—you're not going to get where you want to go.

An ongoing study of young adults finds that only two out of every five members of Generation WTF reported that they have a clear sense of purpose. Yes, you've got some ideas, but perhaps you've never been taught how to formulate goals and make specific plans to achieve your dreams. You've got a general sense of where you want to go, but maybe you've got no clear map. If so it's time to recalibrate your GPS and find your life pupose.

Finding Your Purpose

I grew up with very supportive, enabling parents who
provide for me in every manner to be expected. However,
I am acutely lacking any serious desire to excel in anything.
That's not to say I'm depressed or pathetic, just that I lack
a central motivation or ambition. —*Aaron*

The Skinny on The Road Less Traveled

Most self-help books are markers of short-lived fads, but some, like M. Scott Peck's *The Road Less Traveled*, are credited with inspiring millions. The book spent more than thirteen years—*years*, not weeks—on the *New York Times* bestseller list.

Peck was the last of the twentieth-century self-help giants. Like Dale Carnegie and Norman Vincent Peale, earlier advice-giving legends, Peck, a psychiatrist and a religious speaker, encouraged his readers to take responsibility for their problems and face the unglamorous facts about what life really demands.

In his 1978 guide, Peck told his readers that delaying gratification—scheduling pain first and pleasure later—was "the only decent way to live." The human desire to avoid difficulties and suffering is the root of all mental illness, he argued, and since most of us try to avoid our problems, "most of us are mentally ill to a greater or lesser degree."

Peck's book appeared at a time of high gas prices, economic recession, and plunging housing prices. Sound familiar? The perseverance advice that so deeply resonated during that period of fiscal uncertainty continues to strike a chord. More than a decade after the book's publication, a survey by the Library of Congress and the Book of the Month Club ranked *The Road Less Traveled* number three on a list of books that had made a difference in the lives of their readers—just behind the Bible and *Atlas Shrugged*. And Generation WTF testers called Peck a "personal cheerleader for someone who is going through a tough time." Peck's advice, students said, was "inspiring," "thought-provoking," and helpful for "getting priorities into perspective."

The advice of *The Road Less Traveled* is a combination of religious inspiration, applied psychiatry, and blunt pragmatism. There are no truly "new" ideas in Peck's book, but his timing was perfect: It had

→

been decades since a popular self-help book had linked those often-conflicting points of view. Peck wrote about sacrifice, pain, and suffering—and why they were all good for you. He described life as a "series of problems" where each person's job was to figure out if he wants to complain or do something productive to cope. Section headings include "The Myth of Romantic Love" and "The Healthiness of Depression." It's a classic worth checking out.

A purpose is that final answer to the question of *why*? Why are you doing what you're doing? Why does it matter? Why is it important? Finding your purpose, argues William Damon, author of *The Path to Purpose*, means figuring out what drives you on a daily basis, what motivates you to achieve those immediate goals, and what inspires you to keep going when the going gets tough.

Myriad psychological and behavioral research has found that finding purpose and meaning play significant roles in wellbeing. It turns out that one of the prime predictors of being happy and healthy in old age is whether you had a sense of purpose going through your life.

Purpose can be big or small. Studies show that most people find purpose in their jobs—even if those jobs aren't exactly glamorous. If you wait tables at a restaurant, perhaps you realize that your purpose is to have people leave happier than when they arrived. If you input data, perhaps you realize that the data you are carefully entering affects decisions on a much broader level. As Damon writes, "Noble purpose can be found in the day-to-day fabric of ordinary existence."

Purpose is intentional. Purpose means doing something like you mean it, not just because you're going with the flow. And when you do that, studies find, different parts of your brain are activated, and you start to learn and grow in faster and more efficient ways.

Purpose is the reason for your goals. While goals and motives come and go, your sense of purpose—your answer to the question "why?"—is the end goal that drives them. You might want to do well on a test, or save enough money for a summer in Ghana, but what's the reason for that? To get good grades to go to medical school to help save lives? To save money to travel to learn more about world culture so you can affect global change?

Purpose can change over time—and can evolve. Purpose doesn't need to be something huge like curing cancer or feeding the world's starving. Those are great goals—and do give many people purpose—but anything that you find challenging, absorbing, or compelling, anything that takes you out of your own head and allows you to make a contribution to the greater world around you—that's purpose.

Again, purpose is the "why" behind what you do—and it's probably the most fundamental statement about who you want to be. It's thinking bigger than short-term things like self-promotion, status, and *things*. But if you're like most of Generation WTF, you're getting a bit panicky now. What's *your* purpose?

Three Steps to Digging Up Your Purpose

Step 1: What am I good at?

The first step to figuring out how you can contribute to society is to figure out what you're good at. You might be a great listener, or a great talker. Maybe you can convince a mouse to give up its cheese, or perhaps you are a whiz with numbers. Think of your particular talents and list them here. Be honest, not modest. Be realistic, too. No one else has to see this list unless you want to share it.

My most valuable gifts and talents are

1. _____ .

2. _____ .

3. _____ .

4. _____ .

5. _____ .

Step 2: What can I do with these gifts?

Look at the list above. And I mean really *look at that list*. How can those skills be useful to others? If you're stuck, don't worry about finding one particular career or calling that uses all of your gifts, but instead look at each individually: If you're a good listener, what could you do with that? How could you help others? How could that skill change a person—or a community—for the better?

1. My talent for _____

  could be used to _____ .

2. My talent for _____

  could be used to _____ .

3. My talent for _____

    could be used to _____.

4. My talent for _____

    could be used to _____.

5. My talent for _____

    could be used to _____.

Step 3: What types of careers or activities would I enjoy that would best use some or all of these talents?

Now is the time to get specific and brainstorm. Look at all the uses for all your individual talents: What makes you excited? What do you think would be the most valuable use of your time? Maybe your purpose in life is to have a great family. Maybe your gifts are best used in business, social justice outreach, or research.

Think of this as a variation on the question, "What do you want to be when you grow up?" When you were a kid, you might have said you wanted to be an astronaut or a firefighter—both excellent career choices that have larger purposes attached to their day-to-day routines—but it's likely you were saying that because you saw something on TV that caught your eye, or you wanted to be the hero in a glossy book your dad just read to you. But this time it's for real, and you're mature enough to have listed your honest strengths, and thought about how they might each be useful.

Let's start small: Fill in the blanks here, or go online to www.genera tionwtf.com to print a version of this exercise. Then, put it somewhere that you'll see every day.

In the next WEEK, my purpose will be to _____

_____ .

To achieve that, I will use my gifts for _____

_____

_____

_____

to accomplish these specific goals:

    a. _____

    b. _____

    c. _____ .

In the next YEAR, one of my main purposes will be to

_____ .

To achieve that, I will use my gifts for _____

_____

_____

_____

to accomplish these specific goals:

    a. _____

    b. _____

    c. _____ .

Okay, that felt good, didn't it? So think about that big question again. How could you combine some or all of your gifts into a purpose-filled career or calling?

With proper training and personal dedication, I could see myself doing one of these things in the next ten years.

1. _____

2. _____

3. _____

4. _____

5. _____

Want to Share and Compare Talents with Others?

Go to www.generationwtf.com to join the wise, tenacious, and fearless as they uncover their talents, too.

Putting It All Together:
Your Personal Mission Statement

In *The 7 Habits of Highly Effective People*, Stephen Covey encourages his readers to craft a personal mission statement that will guide their decisions. This statement should be the "basis for making daily decisions in the midst of the circumstances and emotions that affect our lives. It empowers individuals with the same timeless strength in the midst of change." For Generation WTF, creating that kind of personal mission statement is crucial.

Your personal mission statement is a combination of your core values and your sense of purpose that will guide you through the tough career, personal, and financial decisions that lie ahead.

Look back at your values. Look back at your notes on figuring out your short-term and long-term purpose. What does this tell you about who you are—and who you want to be?

Covey compares a personal mission statement to a personal constitution: It doesn't change much over time and it represents our core beliefs. Your mission statement will guide you in making both daily and major life decisions and will empower you to have strength in the midst of challenges.

Here's how to get started:

▶ Think of sentences that begin with "I will . . ." It can be a list or a series of paragraphs.

▶ Take notes for a few days—and add to the mission statement as you work through this book. Post a draft of your mission statement online at www.generationwtf.com to get feedback—and read the mission statements of other Generation WTFers.

▶ After you've written your personal mission statement, make sure you'll be reminded of it in the future. Go to www.generationwtf.com to find out how I can remind you of what you wrote months from now.

Creating a mission statement isn't something that will happen overnight, but it also won't write itself. So use the space on the next page—or the pages in your journal—to think about what you might like to include. Look back to your core values as an early guide.

_____

_____

_____

_____

_____

_____

_____

If this seems a bit challenging, you're not alone: Testers found that this exercise required a good deal of thought. You don't wake up every day with an end-game in mind because "the end"—whether it is the end of the semester, the end of an internship, or the end of your life—seems too far away to easily contemplate. Those who accepted the challenge and drafted a mission statement, though, said it changed the way they approached decisions both big and small.

Thinking about your values, finding your purpose, and crafting a personal mission statement gives direction to your life—and it puts you way ahead of your peers.

"A personal mission statement has helped me because it made me realize what I want in life, how I want to do that, and the reason for what I want in life," said Katherine. "I realized that I want to graduate from college, go to grad school, and get a good job as a counselor. These things can make me a better person. I need to remember that my grades now will affect the future."

A big part of Katherine's mission statement was to focus less on material objects and more on character and happiness. "By not being obsessed by material possessions, [I can] keep my character in check [and stop] worrying if I have the latest iPod."

Crafting a personal mission statement means making a commitment to your values—and beginning to understand your purpose in life. Get started now jotting down ideas and personal pledges, and then, for the next few weeks, as you read and work your way through this book, let it be a work in progress.

A Wise, Tenacious, and Fearless Mission Statement

Ask yourself:

▶ How do I want to live out my values?

▶ How do I want to use my gifts?

▶ How can I best achieve my purpose?

▶ What roles do I serve to others? (Think about your interactions with others as a son/daughter, spouse, friend, and neighbor.)

▶ What do I want to achieve?

▶ What makes me feel powerful, wise, and secure?

Because we're going to be referring back to your values, your purpose, and your mission statement personal promises often, you might want to use this page to copy down what you're thinking so far—so you'll be able to more easily flip back to remind yourself of these values as you work through the rest of the book.

My name is _____ .

Today is _____ .   **I am** _____ **years old.**

My FIVE CORE VALUES are

1. _____ .

2. _____ .

3. _____ .

4. _____ .

5. _____ .

My FIVE CORE TALENTS are

1. _____ .

2. _____ .

3. _____ .

4. _____ .

5. _____ .

In the next ten years, my PURPOSE will be to

1. _____ .

2. _____ .

3. _____ .

4. _____ .

5. _____ .

The key concepts I want to include in a personal mission statement are:

1. _____ .

2. _____ .

3. _____ .

4. _____ .

5. _____ .

Special Online Bonus

After you've drafted your personal mission statement and core values, make sure you'll be reminded of it in the future. Go to www.generationwtf.com to find out more.

chapter 2

Get Honest with Yourself

The WTF Guide to Journaling

In many ways, you are "Generation Direct." You're all about blunt communication and telling it like it is. You seem pretty comfortable critiquing folks older or more senior than you. But how well do you really know yourself? How honest are you about your own strengths and weaknesses?

Now that you're honing in on your values and purpose, ask yourself, "Am I living out my personal mission statement and values on a day-to-day basis?" Honestly? To improve the odds of a resounding "*Yes!*" let's go a little deeper.

Honesty is about internal integrity—internal wholeness. It's about being comfortable in your own skin. Facing some core truths about what is and isn't honest behavior will make you more likely to like what you see when you look in the mirror each morning (moisturizer also helps).

To become a wise, tenacious, and fearless you requires the wisdom of honest self-reflection to learn who you really are. This chapter gives you several different paths to the ultimate wisdom: "Know thyself."

WTF Is Honesty?

Honesty is being worthy of trust. It's being reliable. It's about acting with integrity. As a society, we've tried to encourage these qualities in each generation: Youth programs like the Boy Scouts, the Girl Scouts, and the Children's Defense Fund offer activities to encourage honesty as a character trait. And repeated research suggests that authenticity may be coachable well past those formative years. From spiritual practices to psychotherapy to inspirational self-help books, we continue to try to teach the virtue of honesty even into adulthood. Translation: It's not too late to get honest with yourself.

On the face of it, we take honesty really seriously from the beginning. Parents teach honesty by what they say to their children. If the punishment for lying is more severe than the penalty for telling your parents what you did wrong, you'll be more encouraged to be honest.

But parents also teach honesty (to a greater or lesser degree) by their own actions. Tell your grandmother that you love the gift she gave you, a parent might say, when the truth is that you hate the fleece night-gown. Do as I say, not as I do. Early on the messages we receive about honesty are conflicted—honesty in some situations is rewarded, while "white lies" are encouraged in others.

And as you get older, the gray area between those white and black lies becomes even more confusing: Should you honestly tell your room-mate she looks fat in her summer white pants, or that he should dump his clingy girlfriend? Where is the line between direct communication and hurtful, unnecessary insults? Telling it like it is might not be based in honesty at all—but rather in driving people apart in distrust and anger—while empty flattery surely isn't being true to your feelings.

Formulaic friendliness will make anyone cringe, and blunt honesty can become brutal honesty pretty fast.

Somewhere along the line, honesty became the antonym of politeness. Thinking of others' feelings became a sign of being out of touch with your own. All of a sudden it seems that to be honest means admitting how bad things are. If you are happy, perky, or positive, you must be lying to yourself. And this is a problem for young adults. Honesty has morphed "into the mockumentary tone of MSNBC and Comedy Central shows—as if anyone who claims to be doing good must be lying, and all sacred cows deserve to be torn down, disproven and laughed at," Phil Fox Rose, a young adult commentator, recently told me.

To get back on track means taking a good hard look at yourself and embracing the power of *real* inner honesty.

Honesty with Yourself

Internal or self-honesty means discovering, acknowledging, and then following your true values.

- ▶ Do you make excuses for your behavior, even when you know you've acted inappropriately?
- ▶ Do you suppress your feelings or overreact to life's problems?
- ▶ Do you wonder where your time goes or feel out of control in your spending?

It's time for some inner honesty and self-reflection. Current popular psychology focuses on gaining inner honesty first as a stepping-stone to external honesty toward others. Or, to paraphrase one cultural philosopher, before you can say, "I love you," you must first learn how to say the "I." That is the only way you can have honest dealings with yourself and others.

Throughout this book, there are surveys to help you learn about yourself. They aren't the usual "quizzes" you see in self-help books. These are psychological inventories that should help you get a sense for how you see the world and where you might be able to improve a bit.

And while psychological surveys are interesting on a general level, to explore inner honesty is a much more personal exercise. Generation WTFers tested out honesty advice from a handful of self-help guides. Their conclusion? Start writing. You like to share on paper, in texts, or online—so put those skills to good use.

Generation WTF Gets Honest

"When I think of honesty, I think of integrity, confidence, being bold, and valuing the realities and facts of life even when they are difficult to face. Living life as an honest person is not as simple as people would like it to be. For instance, being honest with one's own self is one of the hardest things to do, especially when a person encounters a life-changing experience or has to admit their own faults." —Gina

"A person that lies to themselves will never truly understand themselves and then others will never be able to. People may be able to convince themselves that something is true, even though it is not, and in the end cause a whole line of betrayal." —Sara

"Self-reflection requires us to realize something about ourselves that we may not even know." —Emily

Top Honesty Advice: Grab a Journal

Get to inner honesty fast—with a good old-fashioned paper and pen. Or laptop. Or tablet computer. Just start writing in whatever confidential format that makes you feel comfortable. There are four types of journals you can choose from to get you focusing inward:

1. A time journal,
2. A tough-love journal,
3. A gratitude journal, or
4. A money journal

Read about each, figure out which one seems best for you right now . . . and commit to trying it for a week. Then, go back and try each one that grabs your attention. Do them all and make the next month one of honest self-awareness.

How Many Times a Day Do You Lie?

We all know it's bad to lie, but we do it anyway. One study suggests that the average person tells four lies each day—or nearly 100,000 times in a lifetime. The most common lie is "I'm fine," reported the British newspaper, the *Daily Mail*. Other popular lies included, "Sorry I missed your call," "Our server was down," "Nice to see you," and "I'll call you back in a minute." Sound familiar? Have you used one of these in the last twenty minutes, perhaps?

Most Common Generation WTF White Lies

Age ("Yeah, I'm 21.")

Hair color ("I'm a natural strawberry blonde.")

→

←

Why you're late ("There was an accident on the highway and the traffic was terrible.")

Whether you were in class ("I've been to every lecture . . . I sit in the back, so maybe you didn't see me?")

Your hygiene ("Yes, Dr. Dentist, I brush and floss daily.")

Your possessions ("I swear it's not mine, officer.")

Your friends ("Your hair looks fine . . . no, that tube top doesn't make you look fat.")

Not-So-White Lies We Tell Ourselves:

"Whatever . . . the grades I get in college don't matter. It's about living for the moment."

"You don't need to say 'thank you' for things that you deserve."

"Everyone cheats. And copying a homework assignment isn't *really* cheating."

mm

1. The Time Journal: How Do You Really Spend Your Time?

For one week, write down everything you do—and how long it takes you to do it for. How long do you spend at work or studying? How long at the gym? Online? E-mailing? Going out? Watching TV? Playing video games? In her 2010 book, *168 Hours: You Have More Time Than You Think*, Laura Vanderkam challenges readers to honestly track what they do in a week . . . and then see where they can use their time in ways that better reflect their goals and values.

Most of us have no idea where our time goes, she argues—and that's the main reason we think we're so busy. We tend to underestimate how much time we sleep and hang out relaxing, and overestimate how much time we spend working or doing chores. But knowledge is the first step to gaining power over your schedule. To make this work most effectively, go to www.generationwtf.com and print out schedules that look like the one on the following page.

Yes, the day is broken into thirty-minute slots. But being a little compulsive about your time will have eye-opening benefits: If you do it for one week, you'll get an honest estimate of where you are focusing your time.

Among the key points to maximize the benefits of your time, according to *168 Hours*:

Figure out where your time goes. Use a timesheet for a week— and be honest!

Figure out your core competencies. A core competency is something only you can do, or something that you do particularly well. What can be done only by you every week? For example, only you can spend that quality time with your best friend. Only you can get yourself in shape. And only you can do certain projects at work or at school. If you invest your time on those core competencies, you'll be more efficient—and feel more satisfied by your efforts.

Do work that makes you happy. Being happy in your chosen work allows you to get into that great "blissed out" work zone where you are totally absorbed in what you're doing and actually accomplishing a lot and doing it more efficiently than if you were dragging your feet.

Watching TV is not the best use of your leisure time. Americans watch, on average, about thirty hours of television each week. But studies show vegging out in front of the TV doesn't give us as much

	MONDAY	TUESDAY	WEDNESDAY	THURSDAY	FRIDAY	SATURDAY	SUNDAY
5AM							
5:30							
6							
6:30							
7							
7:30							
8							
8:30							
9							
9:30							
10							
10:30							
11							
11:30							
12PM							
12:30							
1							
1:30							
2							
2:30							
3							
3:30							
4							
4:30							
5							
5:30							
6							
6:30							
7							
7:30							
8							
8:30							
9							
9:30							
10							
10:30							
11							
11:30							
12AM							
12:30							
1							
1:30							
2							
2:30							
3							
3:30							
4							
4:30							

pleasure as an evening with friends or spending quality (focused) time with family.

Take control of your calendar. As Stephen Covey argues in *The 7 Habits of Highly Effective People*, we often spend too much time on the *urgent* matters of life—reading and answering the e-mails that ping in, dealing with minicrises, and attending to things that are distracting us—rather than focusing enough attention on the *important* elements, like spending time with those you love and setting and accomplishing career goals. Look through your time diary and be honest about how much time you are currently devoting to "important" stuff.

And what happens if, after doing your time chart, you're not pleased with your reflection? The rest of this book will help you re-prioritize as necessary.

2. The Tough-Love Journal: Be Brutally Honest— and Make a Commitment to Change

In addition to the core guides, Generation WTF testers tried the tough love dished out by Dr. Phil McGraw in his 1999 bestseller *Life Strategies*. Calling the advice "brutally honest" and raving about his ability to "blow people away" with a hearty dose of reality, many WTFers embraced the "get-off-your-ass and do it advice" as "a blunt wake-up call" that "doesn't pull any punches."

He suggests starting a confidential journal in which you have the "freedom to be totally honest." At numerous points McGraw asks readers to be "brutally honest" about their failures and their justifications for less-than-satisfactory outcomes. He routinely suggests that if a person doesn't admit to at least occasionally having a problem with self-confidence, happiness, or decision-making, then that person isn't being honest. "If you are honest, I wager you will admit that you are 'life lazy.' For example, you never take the mental and emotional energy to sit down and write out a goal and a plan to get that goal. You may intend to, but you let yourself slide." (Chapter 3 will help you fix that particular problem, by the way.)

The rewards of honesty are high, he writes:

> If you hope to have a winning life strategy, you have to be honest about where your life is right now. . . . By being honest about your own behavior, you can win tremendous credibility, and foster an environment conducive to change.

Honesty—facing hard truths, uncovering old wounds, and knocking down old barriers—is the only way forward. He counsels:

> Your life is not too bad to fix, and it's not too late to fix it. But be honest about what needs fixing. . . . Be honest, or you will cheat yourself out of what may be the best chance you've ever had to escape the shadows of your current life and to get what you really want.

Sound good? Journaling is something that many psychologists recommend—and it's something that Generation WTFers embraced immediately. Start by asking yourself what you want to improve about yourself. What is working—and isn't—about your life? As the words tumble out, think in terms of specific challenges and solutions.

3. The Gratitude Journal: Honest-to-Goodness Happiness

While writing down your failures and problems may spur you into action to fix them, it's not going to make you immediately happier,

Why Journaling Works for Generation WTF

"We are a therapeutic generation that loves to record. People are constantly updating Facebook, revealing personal happenings or goals. And blogging. So writing things down is a natural way to make changes." —Sara

researchers find. What does seem to make people happy is journaling about the good things in their lives—what makes them feel loved and proud, and memories of happy times in the past.

Keeping a gratitude journal encourages people to exercise more, make more progress toward achieving important personal goals, feel better about their lives as a whole, and express more optimism about the near future, researchers at the University of California, Davis and the University of Miami find. Those who journaled about complaints, hassles, or just the neutral facts of their day didn't get those benefits.

In 59 *Seconds: Think a Little, Change a Lot* psychologist Richard Wiseman offers simple steps to create your own gratitude diary. For five days, write about "topics that will create a happier future": On Monday, write about things for which you are grateful. On Tuesday, write about some wonderful experiences in your life—times when you felt loved or contented, and describe how you felt at the time. On Wednesday, write about what the future might look like if you achieved your goals. On Thursday, write about someone important to you—write him or her a letter about why you care about that person. On Friday, review the previous week and write about three things that went really well for you.

WTF Tips for Great Gratitude

- ▶ **If you're having a gloomy or crabby day, try brainstorming** on what you'd put in your gratitude diary to lift your mood on the spot. "I found myself brainstorming during the day, prior to actually writing things down, about things that made me happy or grateful. I was able to slow down and actually appreciate many of the things I believe I was meant to revel in," Lauren said.

- ▶ **Don't wait until the end of the day** to write things down. If you do your gratitude journaling earlier in the day, you'll get the happy boost all day long.

- ▶ **Thinking of more bad than good things?** Keep trying. This is why the exercise works—because it refocuses your thinking. Emily said, "It breaks the tunnel-vision aspect of our lives."

- ▶ **Feeling anxious?** Try this sort of affectionate writing. "As skeptical as I was, after just a few days, I felt calmer and happier," Nick said.

- ▶ **Carrying a heavy burden?** This might lighten the load. Katherine said, "It helped me feel more positive and present. I tend to go over things that I feel I could have done better that day, which leads me to feel stressed. After completing this type of diary, I really did feel a little lighter."

- ▶ **Feeling lonely?** Writing about someone you care about can help. Since college and work separated her from her close friends, "I often feel a bit lonely when I remember how deep-knitted my relationships were," said Lauren. "So I appreciated writing to a loved one because it effectively reminded me how truly happy I am to have them in my life."

The Skinny on 59 Seconds:
Think a Little, Change a Lot

Respected psychologist and myth-busting author Richard Wiseman's 2010 book, *59 Seconds: Think a Little, Change a Lot*, claimed to distill the best of psychological research into a user-friendly, fast, and surprisingly simple book for personal improvement. And for the most part, Generation WTF testers were convinced that it did just that.

Wiseman uses academic research to shatter the myth that positive thinking alone will improve your attitude and performance—Norman Vincent Peale's *The Power of Positive Thinking* takes a hit—but presents dozens of studies that support Dale Carnegie's simple aphorisms about smiling and complimenting others as the way to win friends and influence people. He explains why writing down your goals is more effective than visualizing them, why retail therapy doesn't actually make you happy, and why active listening in relationships might not be the secret to a happy marriage.

In easy-to-read, quick, and fun chapters (with plenty of interactive exercises), Wiseman explains that spending money on vacations makes you happier than buying a new gadget, expressing gratitude and helping others boost your mood, and finding the silver lining in a situation allows you to come out of a dark moment with your head held high.

▶ **Take your time.** Give yourself some more time when you are writing about your goals. Who knows what you might come up with? Tabatha said, "Thinking about goals for the future not only made me feel happier but more motivated. I took more time writing about this topic because my thoughts led in so many directions: Maybe I'll do this or that, but in the end I felt more confident in succeeding in these goals."

4. The Money Journal: Get Honest about Where Your Cash Goes

A lot of us lie to ourselves about money. Maybe you charge things you can't afford. Or you dread opening the credit card bill because it'll tell you a truth you really, *really* don't want to see.

It's time to get honest with yourself about your financial condition. Compare the money you have coming in and the money you have going out—and be honest enough to "face up to what you are really doing with your money, your thoughts, actions and words," advises financial guru Suze Orman in *The 9 Steps to Financial Freedom*. Sticking your head in the sand might make your mom go away for a bit, but it won't make your money woes disappear.

Money Out

Get out your credit card statements, your bank statements, and any other receipts you can find. Orman recommends finding these records going back two years, but depnding on where you are in life, that might be too much to ask. Go back at least six months—or as far back as you can.

Divide your spending into categories. For some it might be rent, food, going out, gas and car stuff, phone and cable bills, clothing, and travel while others might add books, entertainment, dry cleaning, holiday gifts, or financial aid payments. Use the "WTF Does My Money Go?" worksheet in chapter 6 to help you get started.

Find out how much you spend each month, in each category, by dividing the totals by the number of months you are tallying up. Like it or not, that's how much you spend—on average—each month.

If honesty is the best policy with friends, it's the only way to go with personal finance. Those charges are going to keep adding up, and you've got to start paying down your bills at some point. Sooner is better. Plus, studies show that being honest about financial foibles can get us back on track.

Think something that costs more must be better? According to an economics professor at CalTech, you—and most everyone else—mistakenly do. In a blind tasting of wines, participants rated the higher-priced bottles as more enjoyable. And even brain scans seemed to suggest that they enjoyed the higher-priced wines more. Of course, researchers had passed off a ten-dollar Cabernet Sauvignon as a ninety-dollar bottle, tricking everyone.

Next time you're loving a new gadget or other purchase, consider whether the less expensive one is actually just as good—and remember, your brain will play tricks on you!

Money In

Depressingly, calculating the money you have coming in is always a lot simpler—because there are many fewer sources.

Write down all the income you've got coming in. Look at your

Want to Learn More about Money Honesty?

For a more detailed version of this exercise, see chapter 6.
Go to pages 158–61 for a worksheet on calculating where your money really goes—and whether your spending matches your values.

monthly paychecks (after taxes, alas), any money you get on a regular basis from your parents, scholarship or financial aid income, freelance or part-time work that you do on a regular basis, or any loans. Be sure to write down your after-tax income, because Uncle Sam will take his share.

Divide that number by the number of months you're tallying up. That's how much you've got coming in. And if the amount you've got coming in isn't more than the amount you've got going out, that explains your credit card debt. Chapter 6 will help you rethink your spending.

Honest Money Tip

Try this: If your parents still help you out financially, try opening a separate checking account and depositing your paycheck—or a certain amount of it—there. Sam said this reduced the temptation to ask her parents for more financial assistance. Each week, she calculated what she'd earned and what she'd spent. She circled the unnecessary expenses on her receipts and kept records in a folder. By the end of the month, she was saving more and realized she'd overestimated her cost of living.

Honest Goal Setting

Whichever journaling exercise you chose to do first, as you write you'll be thinking of ways to improve—and goals that you want to accomplish to make your life better. The next chapter will help you set SMARTER goals, so that you can put your values and honest self-reflection into action.

WTF Did I Just Learn?

Congratulations! You passed the first stage of the WTF transformation. If you examined your values and considered your purpose, if you got honest with yourself through at least one of these journaling exercises, and if you're excited to apply this knowledge to your life . . . *you just got Wise!*

Here's a quick review:

Values. Values are what's most important to you. Values are about who you want to be. Your values guide your decisions, both big and small.

Purpose. Your purpose is what drives you on a daily basis to achieve immediate goals and keep you inspired for the future. A purpose is the answer to the question "why?" Why are you doing what you're doing? Why does it matter? Knowing your personal purpose gives meaning to life.

Personal mission statement. Your personal mission statement is a combination of your core values and your sense of purpose that will guide you through the tough career, personal, and financial decisions that lie ahead.

Internal honesty. Self-honesty means discovering, acknowledging, and then following your true values. It means not making excuses for your behavior or overreacting to life's challenges. And journaling is a great first step to internal honesty.

Questions to ask yourself:

▶ What drives me? What are my *core values*—and what do I want to do with my skill sets?
▶ What is the *purpose behind my goals*?
▶ What are some of the most important elements of my *personal mission statement*?
▶ How do I *spend my time and money*? Am I able to *give great gratitude*?
▶ Did I really do the exercises?

If you haven't committed to trying at least one of these journaling exercises, flip back to p. 39 and make your selection: *Only you can give yourself a gold star for being Wise.*

GET TENACIOUS

part ii

chapter 3

Got Goal?

The SMARTER Way to Achieve

Generation WTFers repeatedly told me that organization and life balance were their top personal challenges. Indeed, it was out of those discussions that the idea for this book was born. This chapter will help you figure out your goals—and then offer a step-by-step plan to success—tested and approved by your peers.

Why Do I Need Goals?

No one just goes for a walk and ends up on the top of Mount Kilimanjaro. You don't just wake up one day and run your own business. How likely would it be for you to lose thirty pounds, get into graduate school, or make enough money to retire unless you *tried*?

Think of a more basic example: Google is a goal-oriented search engine. It helps us find what we are looking for—to achieve a small goal of knowledge. But you need to be searching for the right terms to find what you are looking for.

Goals give us a direction and a focus for our energies. And accomplishing small goals can create the confidence we need to pursue larger ones.

Goal-oriented thinking helps you take control of your life. It shows you're an adult, willing to accept responsibility for your actions. By setting goals you are saying to yourself and the world around you, "I can accomplish this. I can make a difference."

Goals 101

When you take steps toward accomplishing something you want, you are pursuing a goal. You might start with a desire—a fuzzy idea of what you'd sort of like to see—but when you think about actually making it happen, it becomes a goal. Many goals start off as broad, general, and abstract. You want to retire with a million dollars. You want to learn pottery. You want to lose weight.

In chapter 1, you laid out your purpose. You pondered what you wanted friends and family to say about you after you were dead and gone. Those values are the big-picture ideas that guide you to your goals. In chapter 2, you got honest about where you are right now, what's working and what's not. In this chapter you're going to take those fuzzy ideas of things you like to see happen and turn them into reality.

Let's say one of your values is security—and in your reflections, you've seen that it's an area in which you could improve a bit. What are some goals you might have to really allow yourself to live that value? To achieve financial security, perhaps a goal might be to learn more about paying off your student loans. To achieve personal security, perhaps you'd like to learn self-defense. Now it's your turn. Brainstorm a bit: What are your goals?

_____

_____

_____

_____

Stuck? Go back to page 17 and review your values. Your goals don't have to be huge, although some of them can be big. Think ahead to where you'd like to see yourself a month, six months, or a year from now. What goals would help you get there?

Or, think of it another way: As Stephen Covey puts it in *The 7 Habits of Highly Effective People*, efficient organization and execution of priorities are the way to "run the program" that you have written by setting out your personal mission statement.

Here's what one Generation WTFer's list of goals looked like:

Find a job I like, not just
one to pay the bills

Meet my soul mate

Stop procrastinating

Buy an apartment

Save up money for a trip to China

Lose weight

Not All Goals Need to Be Big . . . Small Challenges Give You a Boost, Too

"I made a list of things that I wanted to do but have put off to see if I could complete everything on my list within a week. For example, updating my resume, organizing my closet, and hanging up pictures that have been sitting in my hallway. At the start of the week, I was focused and began scratching things off my list quickly. I noticed my drive and motivation was high for the thrill of me completing the task, which also made me feel happier throughout the week. After I reached my goal and completed everything on the list, I realized that with a little time put aside for planning ahead, it gives you the motivation you need to follow through." —Tabatha

The SMARTER Plan for Success

I spent a decade analyzing self-help books on motivation, success, and achievement. Along the way, I also scoured the psychological litera-ture for proven tips to turn amorphous ideas into tangible realities. Since the 1960s, researchers have been studying the impact of setting goals on our behavior and achievement—so there's some good stuff out there.

One of the most popular goal-setting acronyms out there is SMART—the mnemonic to remember that goals should be specific, measurable, attainable, relevant, and timebound. Self-help books like Kenneth Blanchard and Spencer Johnson's *The One-Minute Manager* embraced this concept, as have business management programs across the country.

I took the research and offered it to my team of Generation WTFers, who followed variations of this advice and tweaked it a bit themselves. With their detailed feedback, I created a WTF-specific checklist for success. This isn't the traditional goal-setting program you'd learn in a management class, but it is one that's specifically tailored for your generation.

Think of it this way: You are **SMARTER** than the average person. (That's not going to be a stretch for you to remember, I'd imagine.)

To achieve your goals, you need to make them **S**pecific and **M**easur-able. You'll want to take some time to **A**nticipate success and **R**ecord your ideas and challenges. Your goals need to be **T**rackable—using a planner or calendar to set dates for completion—and you'll want to **E**xplain to others what you hope to achieve. Finally, along the way, you'll want to **R**eward yourself for your accomplishments.

"Victory belongs to him who has the most perseverance."
—Napoleon

Create Lasting Change the SMARTER Way

In times of economic trouble, self-help gurus and hot-off-the-press advice books are full of quick-fix advice. But none of that advice works. Personal change takes effort. And just the fact that you've purchased this book (and read this far) tells me you've got what it takes.

So while you aren't Napoleon, the good news is that **intentional changes**—changes you make in your behaviors because you really want to improve, as opposed to changes you make because someone is forcing you to do so—are the ones that last.

How does one change intentionally—and effectively? "A jug fills drop by drop," the Buddha is quoted as saying. And that is perseverance and tenacity in the practical sense. It's the steady persistence of a goal in spite of difficulties, obstacles, or discouragement. Change ain't easy. It takes grit—or "stick-to-itiveness"—the doggedness to stay on task and refuse to stop.

As a child, you were taught to "get back on the horse" and that failure is when we stop trying to succeed, right? The same lessons apply in any behavioral change: Just thinking about a goal isn't perseverance—you have to take action.

Only you can change you—and in the next few pages, you'll be armed with the most effective tools for goal-setting and personal change.

Be SMARTER:
The Generation WTF Checklist for Success

S   Specific: Write down a specific goal.
Writing helps you focus on what *specifically* you want
to accomplish.

M   Measurable: Break that goal into the necessary steps.
Ask yourself questions like "How will I know when I've
accomplished this step?"

A   Anticipate success.
Think of the benefits of achieving the goal.

R   Record your ideas and challenges.
Journaling helps you create a story line and order to your goals.

T   Track your progress.
Use a calendar to plan out your time and chart your path.

E   Explain your goals to others.
By sharing your goals with others, you can ask for help and be
held accountable.

R   Reward yourself along the way.
Give yourself gold stars for each little victory.

The SMARTER Plan in Action

S *Specific: Write down a specific goal.*

Psychologist Albert Bandura finds that people are more likely to want
to accomplish a goal that is specific. When it's clear what we need to
achieve to be successful, we're more likely to act. And the very best
way to push ourselves to get specific is to start writing.

Looking at your list of goals on page 56, pick one to use to put through the SMARTER goal checklist. For example, if your goal was to lose weight, it's time to be more specific. You might say you want to lose fifteen pounds.

My specific goal is to _____.

M *Measurable: Break that goal into the necessary steps.*

To achieve a long-term goal, we need immediate steps, or subgoals, to achieve; otherwise we'll put off doing anything at all. So taking a specific goal and breaking it into a few different steps helps us get started immediately. You can think of it as minideadlines or minihurdles. But spending time at the beginning to lay out the steps to success really does work: In his book 59 *Seconds*, psychologist Richard Wiseman described two large-scale studies he conducted on motivation. By breaking down a goal into a series of subgoals, Wiseman found that people were able to "remove the fear and hesitation often associated with trying to achieve a major life change."

So, sticking with the weight loss example, there could be several steps:

- ▶ Read a book about healthy weight loss
- ▶ Set up an online program to track calories consumed and burned
- ▶ Meet with a personal trainer to craft an effective workout routine
- ▶ Go to the gym five days a week
- ▶ Print out the calorie-content listings of your favorite lunch spots and so on.

For each step, ask yourself "How will I know when I've accomplished this step?" That will make your subgoal measurable, which psychologists find is a key ingredient for success.

To accomplish my goal of _____
I will take the following steps:

Step to Success

_____

     →**I will know I've accomplished this step when . . .**

_____

_____

Step to Success

_____

     →**I will know I've accomplished this step when . . .**

_____

_____

A *Anticipate success.*

You're doing a lot of work—so don't forget what you're working for. Anticipating success is an important step, researchers find. Believing you are capable of success gives you the push to actually go out and do it. If you think of the benefits of achieving your goal—and really believe that you can do it—you're more likely to succeed.

Anticipating success is different than amorphous positive thinking: Rather than simply hoping or praying for an outcome, anticipating success means thinking about the very possible—and likely—good things that will come from your efforts.

If you're trying to lose weight, think about how great you'll look in that smaller size dress or pants. Think of how jealous your ex will be when you go home for the holidays looking so hot. Do whatever you need to do to see it and taste it. Look toward the future and anticipate success.

When I accomplish my goal of _____

I will feel good about _____

_____

_____.

R *Record your ideas and challenges.*

Journaling helps you create a story line and order to your goals. But just writing about how you *should* do this or you *want* to do that won't get you anywhere. Be more specific. Go to www.generationwtf.com to take a character strengths test that will help guide you. After answering all the questions (and there are a lot—but it's a cool exercise), you'll see your signature strengths. Perhaps one of your strengths is leadership. How can your leadership be put to use in accomplishing this goal? Bonus: Researchers have found that people who took this test and used one of their signature strengths in a new and different way for a week boosted their happiness for a month.

Don't want to go online for some serious self-reflection? Then just think about what you're good at—and then think about how, specifically, you can apply those skills to your goal.

So, let's say you're a good cook. That can help with your weight loss goals because you'll be able to find recipes that both taste good and are calorie-friendly. Plus, it'll be fun to use those culinary skills—and kitchen gadgets—that were getting rusty. Review that list of your gifts on page 25 for more ideas.

Now that's not to say that there won't be some challenges—and you can acknowledge those, too. Thinking about your values is useful here, too (again, you'll find them in that handy dandy sheet you created at the end of chapter 1 on page 32):

How will your core values and character traits help you overcome obstacles to achieve your goal?

_____

_____

_____

_____

_____

_____

The Skinny on Samuel Smiles and Self-Help

British author Samuel Smiles gave his seminal 1859 book *Self-Help* the subtitle "With Illustrations of Conduct and Perseverance" because he believed that grit was necessary for all self-improvement. By highlighting examples of "great, but especially good men" to serve as "helps, guides and incentives" to his readers, Smiles teaches the importance of virtuous living. To expand the audience of his advice, Smiles assures the reader that these great men come from colleges, workshops, and farmhouses—from the huts of poor men and the mansions of the rich.

Achievement of all sorts, Smiles argues, takes four key elements: individualism, discipline, the ability to overcome adversity, and a continuing desire to learn. And while Smiles might not know what to make of the SMARTER strategy for goal setting, he would be thrilled to see that his core concepts live on in a modern context 150 years down the road.

T *Track your progress.*

One of the most common problems with achieving goals is actually sticking to them—and accomplishing what we need to, when we need to get it done. We say to ourselves, "No worries, I don't have to think about that yet, I'll have plenty of time to do it later" and forget about our goals. Or, in our more panicked moments, "It's an enormous project, the deadline is looming, but I don't even know where to begin"— and then we just worry, in a state of paralysis.

Behavioral economists and psychologists call this "hyperbolic discounting." It's our tendency to prefer smaller payoffs now over larger payoffs later. And this bad habit means that we're constantly disregarding the future when it requires sacrifices in the present.

It turns out that hyperbolic discounting is the same logical flaw that causes people to overcommit their future schedules; research has found that most people will make commitments long in advance that they would never make if the commitment required immediate action.

Overcoming Adversity

True tests of grit often begin with heart-wrenching adversity. In *Self-Help*, Samuel Smiles shows readers that it ain't as bad as it could be by telling the story of John James Audubon, the ornithologist who catalogued and painted hundreds of birds and wildlife images. Audubon went on a month-long trip and stored hundreds of his drawings in a wooden box, which he left under the watchful eye of a relative. Smiles quotes Audubon:

"When I returned, after having enjoyed the pleasures of home for a few days, I inquired after my box, and what I was pleased to call my treasure. The box was produced and opened; but, reader, feel for me—a pair of Norway rats had taken possession of the whole, and reared a young family among the gnawed bits of paper, which but a month previous represented nearly a thousand inhabitants of air. The burning heat which instantly rushed through my brain was too great to be endured without affecting my whole nervous system. [But after a few days] I took up my gun, my notebook and my pencils, and went forth as gaily as if nothing had happened. I felt pleased that I might now make better drawings than before; and ere a period not exceeding three years had elapsed, my portfolio was again filled."

The lesson Smiles imparts to his readers is clear: If successful men like Audubon can overcome such intense adversity and go on to be successful, so can you. Your goals are attainable with some old-fashioned grit . . . and a SMARTER plan for success.

The cure is fairly simple: From big lifetime goals, to projects due next month, setting goals and timelines—and then working backward to set smaller deadlines along the way—is the surest path to success.

This is where you can harness the awesome power of your planner: Use a calendar to plan out your time.

1. **Get out a calendar.** (You can download a template on www. generationwtf.com)
2. **Set your ultimate deadline**—perhaps something like "Project Due to Boss on January 20."
3. It's early November, and that project deadline seems eons away. But what specific steps do you need to take to accomplish it? **Break it into at least five steps**—probably more.
4. Then, working backwards, **figure out deadlines for each individual step**.
5. **Need some more guidance?** There's an appendix at the back of this book that includes a detailed description of my Advanced Calendar Strategy, where you'll see a sample calendar I created based on some of my own planning in graduate school. Then go to www.generationwtf.com to print your own calendar.

E *Explain your goals to others.*

Sometimes it takes a village to help you achieve your goal. By sharing your goals with others, you can ask for help and be held accountable. You also get kudos from others as you progress toward your goal. From weight loss to getting a big project across the finish line, telling friends and family about your goals—and even employing the buddy system— will help you get where you want to be. (In the next chapter, you'll learn more about the psychology of how this works.)

You Don't Have to Be a Genius to Be a Success

It's grit—not brilliance—that predicts greatness, studies show. From a mid-century longitudinal study of gifted children to a 2007 study of IQ and success, grit has consistently been identified as a predictive measure of success. A now-classic study of violinists in Berlin found that daily "deliberate practice," approximately 10,000 hours worth, made a musician excel beyond his similarly talented peers. In his 2007 book *Outliers*, Malcolm Gladwell extends this principle of 10,000 hours to computer programmers, artists, and athletes. When Albert Einstein quipped, "It's not that I am so smart, it's just that I stay with problems longer," he summed up these findings quite well.

Added bonus: When you explain to others what your goals are, you'll not only get reinforcement (probably—unless you have slacker friends, in which case, they aren't going to be helpful to you right now) but you'll be forcing yourself to clearly and specifically articulate what you hope to achieve . . . and how.

To accomplish my goal, *this week* I will tell the following people about my plans:

_____

_____

_____

R *Reward yourself along the way.*

One of the worst parts about "the real world" is that, a lot of the time, you have to work for no particular reward. Your mom isn't going to tell you she's proud of you when you clean your room . . . in your apartment two hundred miles away. No one is going to give you an A when you pull an all-nighter on the last-minute project your boss assigned. You might get a "hey, thanks," but most of us feel like we deserve something more.

Part of being an adult is rewarding yourself. So as you plot out all this hard work to achieve your goals, give yourself gold stars for each little victory. In my house, we call them "incremental celebrations." Nothing big or fancy, but just a little pat on the back for yourself. If you're trying to lose fifteen pounds, and you're down five pounds on schedule, perhaps you reward yourself with a movie night (and skip the gym).

You can think of rewards any number of ways. In Stephen Covey's *The 7 Habits of Highly Effective People* his final step is to "sharpen the saw."

A woodcutter has been chopping wood for hours and isn't getting very far. Stop and sharpen your saw, a friend advises. No, the woodcutter says impatiently, I'm trying to chop wood here! Covey uses this allegory to demonstrate the importance of renewal—and little rewards of rest or fun—during the self-improvement process.

Physical, social/emotional, mental, and spiritual renewal are all necessary on a regular basis to be an effective person, Covey advises. Giving yourself little rewards along the way is similar. Indeed, psychologist Richard Wiseman found that small rewards, personally set by the participants themselves, gave people in his study on motivation and goal achievement something to look forward to—and made them more likely to succeed.

Go back and look at your subgoals—the steps you outlined in the "M" in SMARTER—Measurable. Each time you accomplish one of these steps, what little reward can you give yourself?

Step to Success

→Reward I'll Get When I Accomplish It

Step to Success

→Reward I'll Get When I Accomplish It

I've got a lot going on. I'm balancing a part-time job, graduate-school classes, and I'm trying to find a real job in the future. Oh, and I'd like to still have a social life. But nothing ever seems to get done on time. It's really stressful because I feel like I'm always apologizing or avoiding someone because I was supposed to do something for them. And with big, long-term projects it's the worst. I mean to get it done, but somehow it's always a big drama at the last minute. I've tried to write things down in a planner, but I don't get results. What else can I do? —*Alex*

Reward Yourself with Fun

"Many times it becomes so easy to get wrapped up in your own world full of stress that you forget about the things in life that are fun and make you happy. Going out with friends or simply staying home to relax are good ways in which to renew yourself. Yet drinking and watching TV don't really benefit you physically. I created a list of activities such as jogging, canoeing, riding my bike, and swimming—all activities which I enjoy yet don't find much time in my schedule to do. In high school I was a competitive swimmer, and getting into the pool was an outlet to get rid of frustration, even if I thought practices were going to kill me.

"So by scheduling a chunk of time to devote to getting back in the pool on a regular basis, I rediscovered just how much I enjoy swimming. And truthfully, with summertime and swimsuit season approaching rapidly, my rediscovery couldn't have come at a more appropriate time. The great thing about Covey's advice is that it's very applicable to everyday life. While so much of self-help books require you to think critically about yourself, bad habits, and inner demons, this piece of advice told me to make time for something I love, which makes it very easy." —Liz

When I was a kid, my mother wanted me to learn how to play the piano. I, however, hated to practice. I did every little devious thing I could to get out of it. Lies, diversions, delay tactics, you name it.

So picture little-girl me, say, seven years old, getting called up for a piano recital performance. I hadn't practiced enough. I was nervous. All these people were watching . . . I was going to be terrible. With time, and options, running out, I decided it was time to die: I held my breath as long as I could in hopes that I would pass out—temporarily or forever—and thus get out of the performance.

I rationalized that if I were sick (or dead) I couldn't be held accountable for my lack of practice. So I held my breath . . . and kept holding it . . . and finally gave up. I wasn't going to die soon enough, and people were watching. A clunky Pachelbel's Canon in D Major ensued.

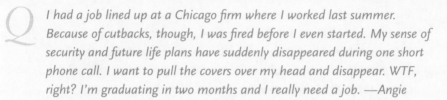

Q *I had a job lined up at a Chicago firm where I worked last summer. Because of cutbacks, though, I was fired before I even started. My sense of security and future life plans have suddenly disappeared during one short phone call. I want to pull the covers over my head and disappear. WTF, right? I'm graduating in two months and I really need a job.* —Angie

A I'm so sorry. Sometimes life just sucks. Things go wrong. As dozens of self-help books will tell you, overcoming adversity is one of the quintessential life experiences. So, congratulations, you're in the game. But that's not a whole lot of comfort, is it?

To find a job takes grit—you've got to send out dozens of resumes, follow up with recruiters, ace interviews, and mine all your connections. Your values and personal mission statement will guide you as you figure out what general career path is best for you. Then, harness that SMARTER system to set clear goals.

During the time I was asking Generation WTFers to try out this advice, Dana was in a similar situation: She needed to get a job ASAP. Perhaps you can try her strategy:

"I decided I needed to apply for two jobs by the end of the first week. . . . Communicating my plan to others greatly increased my success. I told my sister and friends about my goals, and my sister told me about two relevant job openings she'd heard about and my friend took me to an open house. The act of telling others about my motivation plan increased their helpful behavior and helped me in my search."

While you may not have tried to hold your breath to get out of your most recent big, looming project, odds are you've followed a similar (il)logical path.

Say you have a goal to accomplish that's months away. You might take one of three attitudes toward it: In your head, you could say:

1. "No worries, I don't have to think about that yet. I'll have plenty of time to do it later"—and then forget about it.

Q

At my new job, I'm being asked to learn how to work with a specific financial program. I'm not a numbers person at all. I've tried to learn a few times, and I make so many mistakes that I usually give up and do my other work that I'm better at. I want to stay at the company and get promoted, so I've got to learn how to do this. I'm seriously bad at it, though. What should I do? —Sue

A

This is a common story for all of us when we're learning a new skill or trying to change something about ourselves: We expect change to happen immediately—and want to quit trying when it doesn't happen right away.

The bad news is that learning a new skill can take a while and be quite challenging. But here's the good news: Most other people are going to quit, and if you stick to your goal, you're more likely to get the reward.

Want more good news? According to psychologists at UCLA, making mistakes as you learn something actually helps you learn it faster and better. It's the theory of "deep practice": The harder it is for you to learn something, the more your brain is challenged to work in an efficient and useful way. You're more likely to get the skill—and keep it—than someone who thinks it's easy. "We think of effortless performance as desirable, but it's really a terrible way to learn," said Robert Bjork, chair of psychology at UCLA.

---

2. "It's an enormous project, the deadline is looming, but I don't even know where to begin"—and then just worry about it, but not do anything.

3. "What smaller goals do I need to accomplish—and by when—to make sure I meet the big deadline?"—and then work backwards from the end date.

You know the right choice is number three, but I guarantee you that you've taken options one and two in many (if not most) situations in your life.

Why? As human beings, we may be hardwired that way. Being mortal creatures with limited life spans and resources, the human survival instinct has evolved with a basic understanding that you can't enjoy something you've saved up if you're dead. This hardwired tendency may be the bias behind a lot of our short-sighted choices, causing many people to make decisions that lead to short-term happiness and long-term disaster.

Of course, we're not living in the Stone Age anymore. Life-threatening danger does not lurk behind every tree. Sure, you could be hit by a bus tomorrow, but you probably won't be. And while I tried to hold my breath and conveniently pass out to escape from my piano-mortification, those tricks are a lot less cute now that we're adults.

The cure is fairly simple: From big lifetime goals, to projects due next month, setting goals and timelines—and then working backwards to set smaller deadlines along the way—is the surest path to success.

That's where the SMARTER goal-setting plan comes in. Try it (especially the "T" step, where you track your goals and use your planner to the fullest). I think it'll work wonders for you.

Let's take stock of where you are:

▶ You've laid out your values and purpose—and begun thinking about a personal mission statement.

▶ You've gotten honest about what makes you happy and where you could use a little improvement.

▶ You've learned the SMARTER strategy to achieve your goal and chosen a plan to put into action.

And now, of course, you've got to figure out how to follow through and *do it*. We all know how we should behave, it's just the *doing* that dogs us. The next chapter will give you the best tips from decades of psychology and behavioral economics so you can achieve whatever goal you laid out for yourself.

Just so you don't forget what you're working for, remind yourself here:

My top three goals are to:

1. _____.

2. _____.

3. _____.

chapter 4

Self-Control

Your Key to Self-Improvement

When you want to get up for an early flight, what do you do? You set an alarm.

If you want to bench-press your body weight, what do you do? You slowly build up your muscles so you can achieve your goal.

When you've got a big deadline looming, what's the best way to handle it? Plan out your time.

If you're like most people, you *know* all these things are true, but at some point or another, you've dropped the ball: You've missed a flight because you cut it too close, you've overestimated what you can physically do, hurting yourself in the process, and you've tried to cram in a month's worth of work into a frantic forty-eight-hour panic fest. Yes?

You're not alone. Even Aristotle knew this when he said, "I count him braver who overcomes his desires than him who conquers his enemies; for the hardest victory is over self."

You want the secret to success. You want to take control of your life and achieve your goals. We all do. The problem is, of course, there's no one quick fix that's going to get you where you want to go. This chapter is about the proven mental tricks, organizational strategies, and tools to conquer the bored, unfocused, and lazy in all of us.

But first, let's see how you approach work and decision making.

There are no right or wrong answers here, so be honest.

Is the Way You're Working . . . Working?

Directions: Indicate how characteristic or descriptive each of the following statements is of you by using the code given below. Circle the appropriate answer.

  2 Yep, that totally describes me. I strongly agree.
  1 That's on target—most of the time. I agree.
−1 Not really—I don't do that often. I disagree.
−2 That never describes me. I strongly disagree.

1. When I do a boring job, I think about the less boring parts of the job and the reward that I will receive once I am finished.

    2   1   −1   −2

2. When I am faced with a difficult problem, I try to approach its solution in a systematic way.

    2   1   −1   −2

3. I usually do my duties quicker when somebody is pressuring me.

    2   1   −1   −2

4. When I find that I have difficulties in concentrating on my reading, I look for ways to increase my concentration.

    2   1   −1   −2

5. When I plan to work, I remove all the things that are not relevant to my work.

    2   1   −1   −2

6. I often find it difficult to overcome my feelings of nervousness and tension without any outside help.

    2   1   −1   −2

7. I cannot avoid thinking about mistakes I have made in the past.

    2   1   −1   −2

8. First of all I prefer to finish a job that I have to do and then start doing the things I really like.

    2   1   −1   −2

9. Facing the need to make a decision, I usually find out all the possible alternatives instead of deciding quickly and spontaneously.

    2   1   −1   −2

10. When I am faced with a difficult decision, I prefer to postpone making a decision even if all the facts are at my disposal.

    2   1   −1   −2

Scoring:

Tally up your points . . . but reverse the sign on questions 3, 6, 7, and 10. So if you answered with a negative number, make it a positive, and vice versa.

10 and above: You're a take-charge kind of person, eh? You're decisive, focused, and whether you know it or not you're living your life by some basic rules that will help you toward success. Even the best habits can be improved by awareness of what you're doing, so don't skip this chapter. Think of it as a pep talk to keep you headed in the right direction.

0–10: Most Generation WTFers land right about here on this self-control scale: My tester average was about a 3.5. You procrastinate sometimes, but you can also get down to business when you really have to produce. Boosting your ability to control your emotions and learning some simple skills to better organize your time will reap big rewards—fast.

0 and below: Take a deep breath, and let's start with some basics of self-control. Learning how to manage your time, emotions, and attitude will make a huge difference in what you can achieve. And learning these steps now will save you years of heartache in your professional *and* personal life.

The quiz above is an adaptation from a "self-control schedule" first used in the 1980s by psychologist Michael Rosenbaum. Want to take a longer version of the test and compare your answers with others? It's online at www.generationwtf.com.

Want a Marshmallow? The Mischel Experiments

You're four years old. You're put in a room, given a marshmallow—or whatever favorite sweet treat you love—by a man in a lab coat, and told that you've got some choices: The man is going to leave, and you can ring the bell if you'd like him to return so you can eat it. Or, you can wait until he returns on his own, and then you can have two treats.

What do you do? And why does it matter?

Walter Mischel, a Stanford professor of psychology, devised this simple experiment in the 1960s and 1970s and made a fascinating discovery: The choices that children make—some gobble down the marshmallow before even ringing the bell for permission, while others stare at the treat in agony and don't last more than a minute, and still others can patiently wait for fifteen minutes until the experimenter returns—have a big impact on their future success in life.

After tormenting these tykes with treats, Mischel followed up with them throughout their lives: Those who waited for the second marshmallow got higher SAT scores. They achieved more. They were better at paying attention. Children who exhibit more self-control go on to become adults who lead more successful lives.

Professor Mischel argues that intelligence is largely at the mercy of self-control, because even the smartest kids still need to do their homework. "What we're really measuring with the marshmallows isn't just will power or self-control," he said. "It's much more important than that. This task forces kids to find a way to make the situation work for them. They want the second marshmallow, but how can they get it? We can't control the world, but we can control how we think about it."

Just like Odysseus overcame the Sirens' song by tying himself to the mast to prevent himself from succumbing to their music, so too must children—and adults—learn to distract themselves from the less optimal outcome to achieve self-control. Perhaps that means disconnecting from the Internet when you've got a pressing writing deadline, or vacationing outside the service range of your cell phone to get yourself to really relax. Perhaps that means playing with blocks instead of staring at the marshmallow, or going to the library before your boisterous roommates get home looking for a party.

Mental tricks—like visualization and thought exercises—can work wonders to improve a child's self-control, Mischel has found. Pretending that the candy isn't real, but just a picture of real candy, and visualizing an imaginary frame around the picture of the candy allows children who weren't able to control their urge to eat the treat for one minute to patiently wait for fifteen.

This chapter is full of tricks to keep you on track—and help you get double the treats, whatever those "treats" may be.

So, you've guessed it. The number one key to success is self-control.

Disappointed? Yeah, join the club. Self-control is hard, it takes work, and you've got to do it *forever*. But the sooner you start, the sooner you'll see the rewards.

Here are the basics.

What Is Self-Control?

The formal, academic definition says that a person displays *self-control* when, understanding the factors that influence his actions and how he can affect those factors, and without external restraints, he does something that involves lesser or delayed reward, greater exertion, or aversive properties. In practical terms, that means "learning how to use pain and pleasure instead of having pain and pleasure use you." That's the secret to success, according to Anthony Robbins in his 1991 best seller *Awaken the Giant Within*. "If you do that, you're in control of your life. If you don't, life controls you."

Sounds easy enough, but choosing to act in a self-controlled way means not always following your first instinct. Maria, who focused on increasing her self-control during her self-help testing, likened it to the challenge of teaching a new driver not to slam on the brakes when a car is skidding on ice. Your first instinct is to try to slam on the brakes and control the car, but you need to use self-control to override that understandable but unhelpful urge and let the car correct itself. It's hard to do because it goes against our instincts—much like it's hard to turn down a party with friends for a night of boring studying—but it's the right thing to do.

To exhibit self-control, you've got to choose between at least two behaviors that will take you in different directions, and whether you've succeeded or not is determined by societal norms. If a potbelly is a sign of affluence in your society, then you've succeeded in controlling your surroundings so you get enough calories to keep that rotund figure. If thin is in, you and your belly clearly can't control your calorie intake.

The big bummer about self-control is that it's usually not a one-shot deal. It requires continued commitment to your goal. Real personal control means saying no *over and over again* to that extra cookie, partying on a school night, and the like. Behavioral economists call this "intertemporal choice." The decisions you make today impact the tomorrows a long way out, and the costs and benefits may be spread over time. This, of course, makes self-control harder to keep up, because we tend to like to make short-term decisions (i.e., play now, pay later) that don't keep up the bargain of our long-term self-control strategies.

So How Do You Get Self-Control?

Dozens of psychological studies tell us that a successful self-controlled existence is a *skill*—and it gets easier with practice. Plus, just the fact that you've picked up this book means that you've got a desire to improve: The quest for self-improvement is, at the core, a quest to increase self-control. This is a bonus for you because one of the most frustrating elements of self-control research is that people who demonstrate self-control skills are more likely to be self-controlled in the future. Since you're reading this book, you're on the right track.

Self-controlled behavior builds on previous patterns of behavior, and those who have self-control are more likely to value it and seek to increase their abilities. Just like feeling out of control of your life can lead to anxiety and depression, so too can a belief in your ability to take charge of events create an optimistic outlook on the future. This isn't to say that self-control can't be learned, but simply building on what you've got now will pay off in a big way later.

In his 1999 bestseller *Life Strategies*, Dr. Phil (Phil McGraw) tells readers that *existing* is instinctual, but *living* "is the exercise of certain learned skills, attitudes and abilities that you have acquired and honed to a sharp and focused edge." To understand that life is a skill will give you "an incredible edge in the competition of life." Or, as the over-the-top self-help guru on *The Simpsons* quips, ask yourself a simple question: "Are you a human *being*, or a human *doing*?"

Here's a fun fact: New research has found that self-control is contagious. Self-control can spread through social networks, according to University of Georgia psychologist Michelle vanDellen. Volunteers who watched *someone else* exercise self-control—by choosing a carrot instead of a cookie from a buffet of options—scored higher on a later test of self-restraint *themselves*. So did folks who *just talked about* having good self-control. Translation: Choose your friends wisely—and when they exhibit self-control, it'll be easier for you to do the same. And if you set a good example, others will follow your lead.

Seven Steps to Amp Up Control of Your Life . . . Starting *Now*

All of this seems daunting and really un-fun? That's where some lab-tested WTF-approved techniques come to your rescue.

Step 1: Start Talking a Good Game

"Our behavior is a function of our decisions, not our conditions," writes Stephen Covey in the opening pages of the chapter dedicated how to be "proactive"—the first of his 7 *Habits of Highly Effective People*. Proactivity means taking responsibility for your actions and choosing to respond positively. A reactive person says, "I have to do that" or "I must . . ." while a proactive person says, "I will chose the appropriate response" or "I prefer . . ." And while we can't control the world, we can control our reactions and personal choices—or, as Covey calls it, our "circle of influence."

Test it out. For thirty days, watch your language. Try speaking in proactive language that focuses on making and keeping commitments among friends and family.

Instead of saying . . .	*Try saying . . .*
My boss is making me stay late at work.	**I'm going to finish up this project and be home by eight.**
I can't get a job.	**I'm still actively looking for the right opportunity.**

_____   _____

_____   _____

_____   _____

_____   _____

_____   _____

Sounds simple enough, right?

The thirty-day test was more challenging than Sam had expected. However, when she was focusing on her word choice and behavior, she found that choosing proactive language brought about "a new perspective" and helped her calm down when she was stressed or angry.

Fellow tester Victoria said instead of saying "I have work to do so I can't hang out," she began telling her friends, "'I choose to do this first so I'll have uninterrupted time to spend with you later.' My friends appreciated my honesty and explanation," she reported.

You don't have to sound weird and stilted about it either. Use your own words. Just think about whether you're complaining and feeling put-upon, or taking charge of your emotions and choices.

Being proactive with your language means more than just changing words—it's about taking responsibility for your actions in word and deed. Testers accepted Covey's thirty-day challenge and applied proactive approaches to their schoolwork, their job searches, and their friendships. The results were impressive.

Be Proactive in School

Ask for help when you need it. Aly said before reading Covey's advice, she'd never visited a teacher during office hours or asked for help on an assignment. "I don't know if it was because I was being lazy or I would rather do things on my own," she said, but in the final semester of her college career, she decided to give it a try. "I decided to visit some teachers in office hours to get some feedback on what I had been working on and have them clear up some questions [for my final assignments]. It turns out that being proactive with your schoolwork also leads to better grades than I would have thought," she reported. "I should have been implementing this advice in my life for the last four years because it was so simple I just never realized it would be so beneficial."

Take ownership of your academic career. Chris aced his second biology exam after failing the first one, because he studied each night for several weeks to make sure he understood the material. Emily, a fourth-year student who wasn't going to be graduating on time, said Covey's advice helped her channel her frustration about having to take more course credits for graduation into more productive efforts to do well in the classroom.

Own up to your mistakes and take responsibility. Katherine said when she "spaced" on an assignment, she took the proactive approach: Rather than lie or ignore the situation, Katherine "realized that it was just best to tell the professor I forgot to do the assignment and go from there. The professor was understanding and told me to just e-mail it to her. By taking personal responsibility for my actions I did not get into trouble or feel bad because I had nothing to feel bad about. . . . I feel like I was proactive when I did not make up some excuse and just told the plain truth."

Face your fears. For Lindsey being proactive meant getting up the gumption to apply for the selective social work program at the university, even though she was afraid she might not get in. After reading

Covey's advice, she wrote, "You have to create your own path and your own success. You cannot just wait for an opportunity to fall from the sky and hit you on the head, you have to go out and get it yourself." Covey's advice was what spurred her on: It "made me realize that if I didn't even try to get in, a spot that could have gone to me would go to someone else. Because of that, I ended up applying and I just found

---

The Skinny on
The 7 Habits of Highly Effective People

Stephen Covey, a business management professor, had studied effective styles of leadership and organization for more than two decades when he wrote *The 7 Habits of Highly Effective People* in 1989. What made this book such a runaway success—selling more than fifteen million copies in thirty-eight languages—is that it's not just a business book, it's a life-improvement guide that synthesizes some of the greatest virtue-based ideas of American self-help. Covey, who studied 250 years of success literature before embarking on his book, borrows from the great masters of self-help.

Covey argues that before you can achieve greatness within business, family, or your community, you must first find your inner strength and character. While other guides may jump right to quick-fix approaches, Covey says that true change requires a focus on the "character ethic" not the "personality ethic." Character is primary, personality is secondary—and simply to understand that will be a paradigm shift, a new approach or life map, for many readers. "The way we see the problem *is* the problem," writes Covey. Rather than superficial changes, he asks his readers to take a "principle-centered, character-based, 'inside-out' approach to personal and interpersonal effectiveness." And to do this takes self-control and commitment.   →

out this week that I got accepted. That never would have happened if I had not read this book and took Covey's advice."

Be Proactive in Job Searches

Apply early. Lainie said Covey's advice encouraged her to apply for summer jobs earlier than she had in previous years. "I took the initiative and called around, and I ended up finding this volunteer opportunity

---

←

Following this outline, the rest of the book is divided into three sections—personal victories, public victories, and renewal. Habits 1–3 are personal developments toward independence—becoming a proactive person, beginning with the end in mind, and putting first things first. Habits 4–6 are part of the quest for interdependence and good relationships with others—thinking in terms of win/win scenarios, seeking first to understand the other person before seeking to be understood yourself and the ability to synergize, or work together successfully in a group. The final step, and the final section, is about sharpening the saw—continually renewing your most valuable asset: you.

Covey tells readers that to get the most out of his book they should use it as a reference and continually return to the text for a refresher. On the first reading, Covey suggests readers engage with the text as if they were going to have to teach the information to someone themselves within the next forty-eight hours, another good active reading strategy. It's a rousing introduction—and one that inspires readers to make commitments to personal change—but Covey doesn't sugarcoat his message: It's not about lip service to self-improvement, it's about examining your principles and embarking on a drastic personal overhaul.

at a hospital in Chicago that I would not have gotten if I waited any longer," she said, crediting *The 7 Habits of Highly Effective People* for lighting a fire under her.

Make the effort. Alex said rather than wait until after graduation to think about the future, he attended a very crowded university-sponsored job fair. "It looked like the biggest can of sardines in the world. The room was packed shoulder to shoulder and I thought there was no way this would benefit me but I stayed and ended up with an interview. I did learn that job hunting was not going to be easy, and I had just experienced the first step in finding my future career. I didn't expect much, but getting that interview showed that putting in that little effort did pay off."

Follow up. Aly said her mother had been encouraging her to be proactive for years. "She would always say that things are not just going to happen for me and I need to go out and take care of myself. Of course I would just roll my eyes and walk away. However since a self-help guru agreed with her I thought I would give it a shot." Aly focused on her postgraduation job search and started sending out resumes, continuing to apply and follow up even when she got no response. "By being proactive I managed to get an internship for the summer. Stephen Covey's advice of being proactive is really just a reminder to people that you have to help yourself, and again I think it takes a self-help book to be reminded of something so simple."

Be Proactive with Friendships

Choose to be happier. "I used to get really pissed at my roommate who constantly leaves messes," said Chris. "But by applying Covey's advice I realized that I *chose* to get pissed at the messes instead of just asking him to pick up after himself. While there have still been plenty of messes, I have been in a better mood and my roommate has begun doing a little better," he said. Proactivity to the rescue.

Face challenges head-on. Faye said taking a proactive approach to a friendship on the rocks put things back to normal quickly: Through the grapevine she'd heard that a friend was complaining that Faye was "acting poorly towards her, so I took it upon myself to go and talk to her and see what was bothering her. Turns out, it was something recently where she thought I was leaving her out. I was so happy that I went and talked about it with her because usually if I hear something like that, I try to make it better by ignoring the actual situation and just trying to be nicer. This was a new habit that I was going to start doing because my friend really appreciated me coming up to her and trying to make things better," she said.

What are your proactive goals? In the next month, what types of changes—in your language, your attitudes, and your actions—can you make to get proactive in life? Take a minute to list a few proactive steps you can take, starting now.

In the next month I will be proactive about . . .

_____

    →**by doing/saying/acting in the following way:**

_____ .

In the next month I will be proactive about . . .

_____

    →**by doing/saying/acting in the following way:**

_____ .

Master Yourself

"Some people say that you have to like yourself before you can like others. I think that idea has merit, but if you don't know yourself, if you don't control yourself, if you don't have mastery over yourself, it's very hard to like yourself, except in some short-term, psych-up, superficial way," writes Stephen Covey in *The 7 Habits of Highly Effective People*. And achieving this kind of personal control—part of what Covey calls the private victories necessary for success—means accepting responsibility for your actions.

To put yourself in control of your life immediately, Covey says one must "make a promise—and keep it. Or we can set a goal—and work to achieve it. As we make and keep commitments, even small commitments, we begin to establish and inner integrity that gives us the awareness of self-control and the courage and strength to accept more of the responsibility for our own lives."

For Tim, personal responsibility translated to personal rewards. "It doesn't take much energy to delay in doing something in order to finish your goals first, but it really pays off in the end. It helps give an incentive to doing what needs to be done anyway. Rewarding yourself can be a powerful tool in self-change. This type of discipline and self-control takes some effort, but I think it really works."

Step 2: How Much Do You Want It?

How often have you heard a politician promise that "this will be a top priority for my administration"? We roll our eyes when we hear empty promises like that because, seriously, how many top priorities can you really have?

Not that many.

There's a difference between the ideal and the reality of all situations. Similarly, there's a difference between what you can ideally accomplish and what you can actually accomplish.

Commitment to a goal isn't costless. Your choices have consequences, so it's important to choose to commit yourself to something that you really want to do, not something that you feel you ought to do, or that your parents want you to do. (Not quite sure about what you want to do? Go back and review that summary at the end of chapter 1 on finding your values and purpose in life.)

> *"No one can persuade another to change. Each of us guards a gate of change that can only be opened from the inside. We cannot open the gate of another, either by argument or by emotional appeal." —Marilyn Ferguson*

If you have a lot of easy choices—fast food, mood-enhancing drugs, cool gadgets to spend your money on—and you have the resources to get them, the hardest thing is to say *no* and to choose to commit yourself to a larger long-term goal.

Commitment to the future is costly because it asks you to give up some fun now for some reward that you hope you'll get later.

Think about how this applies to your life right now:

My goal is to _____ **by this date:** _____ .
To accomplish that goal I will *choose to do* the following:

1. _____

_____ .

2. _____

_____ .

3. _____

_____.

By choosing to do those three things, I will *choose not to do* the following:

1. _____

_____.

2. _____

_____.

3. _____

_____.

That's some tough love. We want to have it all, but commitment is costly. Is the sacrifice worth it in the long run? If it's the right goal for you, the answer is usually yes. But if it's a goal set for you by someone else, or something you feel like you should do, but don't actually want to do, use this as a reality check to go back to page 56 and reprioritize.

Start small, with a small number of things you'd like to change or improve—and then really commit to them. Then, try employing what researchers call "commitment strategies" to make sure you make the right choices to achieve your goal: Only stock your kitchen with fruits, veggies, and other fresh, healthy foods. Have money automatically withdrawn from your checking account into your savings account each month. Set your alarm clock the night before and put it on the other side of the room so you have to get out of bed to turn it off at 5:00 a.m.

Just don't try to do them all at once.

Step 3: Yes, You're Fabulous, but You Have to Work Hard, Too

People who believe they can change are more likely to be able to actually do so, and they will also be happier people, researchers find. And unless you think your goals can be achieved, what's the point in trying?

But to really believe that you have the skills, you've got to have some **results** to prove it to yourself and others—not just feel-good talk.

While Generation WTFers have grown up with high *self-esteem*, that's different from *self-efficacy*: Self-esteem is about judgments of self-worth, while self-efficacy is about judgments of personal capability. Self-esteem doesn't always get you to your goals. Just because you think you're fabulous doesn't mean you'll buckle down and write a paper with enough time to get an A.

Building self-efficacy means starting small and building up your confidence that you are capable of sticking to personal change. Lizzie tested out advice from *How to Win Friends and Influence People* and found that as she accomplished her initial goals she was more enthusiastic about continuing to learn other tips: When she tried to smile more and act interested at her job, she noticed her commissions went up. "Getting that feedback was really positive—and made me feel like I was making progress. So I tried to read about more people-friendly techniques to try. It's been great for business, but it's also made work a lot more fun, too."

This is where the "M" in SMARTER goal setting comes in—Measurable. Go back to pages 61–62 for a quick review of how to use measurable strategies to build your self-efficacy.

Step 4: Trick Yourself into Self-Control

Can thinking abstractly about a goal or problem actually help your unconscious guide you to increased self-control—without your conscious mind even trying? A 2009 study in the journal *Psychological Science* offers this as a good shortcut when your best attempts at "being good" seem to be failing.

Kentaro Fujita and H. Anna Han, psychologists at Ohio State University, wondered how the unconscious mind helps us make decisions. They concocted an implicit association test as a way of measuring people's unconscious thoughts about eating an apple or a candy bar.

Before testing people on the apple-or-candy question, the researchers split the subjects into two groups—asking one to think about how to have a good relationship in *concrete* terms (*how* we have a successful relationship) and the other group to think about relationships in *abstract* terms (*why* we need to have loving relationships). The topic that they were thinking about didn't much matter—the idea was just to prime the subjects into thinking about things in a concrete or abstract way, because once we're in a particular mind-set, the next question we're presented with is likely to be filtered through that lens: If you are thinking about the "why" and "big" questions of a relationship, abstractly, when presented with a choice of apple vs. candy bar, you'll tackle that question in an abstract way as well.

So what happened?

When participants were thinking in a concrete, low-level way, they chose the apple over the candy bar about 50 percent of the time. But when they were thinking abstractly, they chose the apple over the candy bar 75 percent of the time. It's not a huge difference, but it's a pretty good bump in the right direction—just by thinking in a different way.

Bottom line: Thinking abstractly about the *why*—the purpose, the higher reason, and meaning—for the goal you want to obtain may help you actually achieve it more than simply thinking about the how-t's of getting there. (If this convinced you to go back and give chapter 1 another try, flip back to page 27 to think about your goals and personal purpose.)

Step 5: Know Your Limits

In graduate school, I called my mother, convinced I had mono. I was tired all the time. I was pale and sickly. After I ran through my symptoms, my scientist-mother asked, "When was the last time you ate a hamburger?" I was annoyed: Here I was, sick, and she wanted to plan a menu for me.

Yeah, well, turns out, I was subsisting on Ramen noodles and candy bars and had made myself anemic.

We can run ourselves ragged sometimes. But there's a limit—and part of being an in-control adult is knowing when it's time to recharge your batteries.

What happens when you go to the gym and do a really hard workout—and then someone asks you to lift a very heavy box? You might not be able to heft it up as high as you could have before your workout. Your muscles are tired and they need a break.

Your ability to make good decisions works the same way. Next time you're feeling frazzled, or about to do something that goes against your goals, purpose, and decisions that you've outlined above, HALT. This acronym, popularized by Alcoholics Anonymous, recognizes that self-control will be a lot more challenging if you are

H   Hungry

A   Angry

L   Lonely

T   Tired

So like anyone who is trying to exert control and choose the better option among the lesser temptations, make sure that you're not compromising your abilities by eating a good meal, regaining your calm, reaching out to friends, and getting some rest.

Dog Tired? Time to Recharge

A 2010 study published in *Psychological Science* found that dogs react the same way humans do: If a dog is tired, or has been asked to exert self-control for a long time in a previous test, it is less likely to succeed in the next test of self-control.

Once again, man's best friend reminds us of an important fact of life: Liz said she frequently gets "stressed out about all the little things going on at once" and then "it becomes very difficult to see past the next couple of days because there is just too much going on at once to be able to handle." After bursting into tears in the bathroom when she found out she'd gotten a lower grade than expected on her math exam, Liz realized her stress was impacting her sleep. "Being tired and stressed was blowing everything out of proportion." After a few deep breaths—and a good night's sleep—Liz realized that her professor's advice was correct: there were more tests to come, and she could still salvage her grade.

Bottom line: Once again, man's best friend reminds us of an important fact of life: Context matters. Just like you're not going to have your best workout when you're feeling tired or run-down, researchers find that your capacity for self-control is "impaired" when you're feeling depressed or stressed. But there is hope: Be nice to yourself for a bit and recharge that self-control reserve.

Step 6: It Takes a Village . . . Find One

You've heard that corny saying that two heads are better than one. But when it comes to achieving your goals, exhibiting self-control, and staying on track, research has consistently found that a supportive team, group, or even just the good-old buddy system, is better than going it on your own.

Think about support groups like Weight Watchers and Alcoholics Anonymous. If you want to lose weight or stop drinking, joining these groups means that you:

▸ **Meet other people who want a similar goal.** Knowing that others share you dreams and desires has an encouraging effect.

▸ **Are held accountable for your actions.** Are you losing weight, staying sober, or sticking to your goals? At weekly (or even daily) meetings, these challenges are discussed—and achievements are celebrated.

▸ **Get the congratulations and support of others when you make progress.** You get a "gold star" from your friends—and that makes you want to continue to try to achieve your goal, continue to exert self-control, and keep up your progress.

▸ **See others succeeding as well.** Seeing the achievements of others can make your goals more tangible—and can show you a path to get there yourself.

You can create this kind of success for yourself—by creating your own team or group.

▸ **Tell at least three friends and family members about your goal—and ask them to help you stick to it.** Public humiliation is generally something we want to avoid. And research finds that public commitments to change are a lot more likely to "stick" than private commitments to change. In a 1980s study, researchers found that if a husband-and-wife team both committed to losing weight, they each lost significantly more weight—and kept it off after six months—than if only one spouse decided to change without the other's involvement and support.

▶ **Find a friend that shares the same goal, and do the buddy system.** Each of you can hold the other accountable— and help the other keep focused. I did this when I was finishing my dissertation and a good friend was finishing her first book. Every morning we'd meet at the library, work for the morning, break for lunch, and work in the afternoon. If she arrived on time and I wasn't there, she'd give me a disapproving look when I rolled in. I'd torment her in the same way if she was late. Needless to say, we got a lot more done together than we ever would have apart.

▶ **Get online.** Meet other WTFers who share your goal and will support you along the way at www.generationwtf.com.

Step 7: Create Bright Lines

What's easier—quitting smoking or dieting?

Yes, you might be addicted to the nicotine in cigarettes, but dieting—and keeping the weight off—is actually more of a challenge for most people than quitting smoking, drinking, or another drug.

Why? Because self-control is easier when we have clear, bright lines delineating what we can and can't do. No more cigarettes—ever—is clear. But you can't say no more food—ever. You don't have to smoke to live, so you can cut it out entirely. You do have to eat to live, so you've got to learn moderation, that evil gray area of uncertainty.

Behavioral psychologist George Ainslie has written a lot about the power of bright lines—clear distinctions between what you may and may not do. The techniques of Alcoholics Anonymous are an example of "bright lines": AA tells recovering alcoholics that they cannot even have one drink because their willpower is not flexible in that area. Your will and self-control are most threatened by rationalizations that permit exceptions to the choice at hand. Bright lines stabilize us, Ainslie finds. But all hope is not lost in those gray areas: gaining skill and increased self-control will allow you to negotiate among blurred lines.

Bottom line: Just don't go there on bad stuff. It is easier to avoid temptation than to overcome it, and "effective management of attention" can prevent the problems from starting, finds social psychologist Roy Baumeister and other experts. Setting clear limits enhances your personal control. If you have a big interview tomorrow, it'll be easier to prepare and get a good night's sleep if you don't go out "just for one drink" with friends beforehand. Once you're at the bar, it'll be harder to say no to that second—and third—drink.

Practically speaking, the more you commit to your course of change (and remember, commitment isn't costless) the more you are likely to set up bright lines and strategies to hold yourself to it. So how bad do you want it? Enough to set up some personal "bright lines"? If so, let's do it:

My goal is to _____ .

My bright-line strategy will be to cut out or add the following commitment _____

_____ .

To help me stick to these bright lines, I will enlist the help of

Person #1 _____

Person #2 _____

Person #3 _____

Dieting: A Case Study in the Challenges— and Possibilities—of Self-Control

Dieting is a favorite choice for psychologists studying self-control because it's measurable . . . and it's challenging. To lose weight you've got to burn more calories than you take in. Translation: Eat less and exercise more. And do that consistently for as long as it takes to achieve your goal. And then don't ever go back to your normal eating habits.

So depressing, isn't it?

You want to do it . . . and for a while you'll try, and then . . . ugh. Either you don't lose weight fast enough and get discouraged, or after being "so good" all day long, you're cranky and binge eat in front of the TV to "relax."

Here's why dieting is so hard:

The future seems so far away. Saying no to that piece of chocolate cake now, in hopes of a thinner and fitter you in the future, is hard. Because that thinner you is only in your mind and dreams, while that cake is right in front of you now.

Dieting isn't a guarantee of happiness and success because weight loss might not really be your end goal. Your weight could be a stand-in for another desire. Maybe to be more attractive or more popular with the opposite sex. And alas, losing weight won't get you all the way there.

Dieting requires continuous self-control rather than just a one time "just say no" approach to some tempting treat. Imagine this scenario: You promise yourself you won't have dessert. Ever. But then it's your friend's birthday and you have a piece of cake. Well, hell, you think, I've blown my diet . . . so you have four more pieces of cake. Academic studies find that this is all too common: The larger goal of the diet can be jeopardized by small decisions along the way. In experiments, dieters who feel they have "blown their diet" eat more than nondieters afterward.

Life gets in the way sometimes, making these day-to-day decisions more challenging. Being angry, tired, or lonely can make us want to eat. Dumped by your girlfriend? A plate of wings and beer sounds good. Frustrated at your boss? A pint of Häagen Dazs could be your go-to fix.

You can apply all of the suggestions in this self-control chapter—indeed, in this whole book—to your quest to lose weight. But here are the top tips that worked for Generation WTF testers:

1. Keep a Food Diary

Write down what you ate—and I mean everything. A handful of nuts? Write it down. Three Oreos? On the list. A few nibbles of cheese at an after-work drinks thing? Yup, it adds up.

Keep this list with you. Go online to www.generationwtf.com for a printable pocket-sized chart to help you keep track.

2. Plan for Success

When you commit to your food diary, do it at a time when you expect to be calm, stress free, and ideally not traveling. WTF testers who tried

> ## Track Those Snacks!
>
> Don't wait until the end of the day to write things down—write as you go. It'll help you make better choices toward the end of the day and it will ensure that you don't forget (intentionally or unintentionally) some of your nibbles along the way.
>
> "As I looked at what I had eaten as each day would move on, I became better able to restrain myself based on the list later on in the day, which is often the hardest part of the day for me in terms of making healthy decisions." —Katherine

to keep a food diary over vacations or breaks were much less successful than those who picked an ordinary week or month to monitor their habits.

Jacki said by picking a good month to get started, she was able to keep a workout streak alive. "I have not been satisfied with my physical health for four years now," she said. "I have started to make myself get off the couch and head to the gym. I now work out anywhere from two to four times a week, which is miraculous because I used to spend hours in front of the television."

3. Groups Are Great

Have you ever done an exercise class at the gym? You know that feeling that everyone is staring at you—so you've got to keep stepping with gusto? We tend to perform better when we think others are monitoring our progress, so work out with friends (or in a gym class) and share your dieting goals with others. You can share your food diary online at www

When It Comes to Dieting, Self-Awareness Is Just as Important as Self-Control

"I have struggled with weight and weight loss since I was in high school. I had an eating disorder in high school and because I have come to accept the person I was and the person I am now, and have seen the drastic changes I have made to make sure that never happens again. I am able to talk openly about the matter now. I didn't realize it at the time, but the particular eating disorder I suffered from—exercise anorexia—was an issue of control. At the time, working out obsessively and eating very little had more to do with self-esteem than anything else. Even though my issues with self-esteem have gotten much better, they are still there. . . . The only issue now is that I eat when I am bored. I don't have as much control over my eating habits as I once did. It is difficult for me to control my eating habits and exercise without flashing back to the person I was before and falling into familiar habits. That is the last thing I want." —Kim

.generationwtf.com or find one of the many online dieting resources that seems right for you.

4. Let Technology Help, Too

Via your iPhone you can automatically post how long (and how fast) you ran on Facebook—so all your friends can congratulate you on that seven-minute mile, or tease you if you missed a day. There are tiny pedometers that wirelessly update to your computer, tracking your steps and calories burned. And there are plenty of websites that

How can I keep myself motivated to stick to a diet and exercise plan when I am bored with healthy food and don't feel like working out?
—Siobhan

This is where friends can really help. If it's warm out, skip the gym and go do something fun and active. Play tennis or basketball. Go for a long walk with a girlfriend. If you live with roommates, you can even start a food co-op where each of you takes a turn with the cooking. It's always more interesting to eat something you didn't make yourself . . . and again, you'll be reinforcing good habits by having a friend share the goal with you.

give you the fat-and-calorie breakdowns of most foods you'll eat along the way.

Putting It All Together

Knowing the tools and skills of self-control is absolutely crucial to achieving your goals and making your mission statement a reality. So remember:

- ▶ Self-control is a skill that can be built up like a muscle—in small steps, with rewards along the way to keep yourself on track.
- ▶ By speaking and acting proactively, you can take control of your professional life and interpersonal relationships.
- ▶ All self-control requires commitment—and usually requires giving up something fun. Make sure you are clear about what you want, set some bright lines, and think about whether it's

worth it so you're not blindsided by temptation (or regrets) down the line.

▶ Ask for help—from friends, family members, and co-workers. You're much more likely to stay on track if you've got the support (and watchful eyes) of others egging you on.

▶ Procrastination is a common enemy of self-control, creating a lot of unnecessary stress along the way. Keep reading, because the next chapter is full of tips and research on how to fight that particular beast.

chapter 5

Procrastination and Stress

The Dysfunctional Relationship That's Holding You Back

You've defined your purpose and you've gotten wise about who you are. You've laid out your goals and are psyched up to achieve them in a SMARTER way. You've even learned the psychology of self-control—and how to make it work for you. But unless you are super-self-motivated, two things will happen along the way: You'll procrastinate, and then you'll get stressed out about whether you're actually going to get anything done on time.

Are you a procrastinator? Go online to www.generationwtf.com to test yourself against an academic scale that's widely regarded as the gold-standard for procrastination research, and find out. It asks questions like "I often find myself performing tasks that I had intended to do days before," "When travelling, I usually have to rush in preparing to arrive at the airport or station at the appropriate time," and "Even with jobs that require little else except sitting down and doing them, I find they seldom get done for days."

If you're a procrastinator, you're not alone.

Do You Procrastinate?

While many of the Generation WTFers I surveyed seemed to do just fine on these procrastination scales, there were two questions that were very telling. Circle your choices below.

I generally delay before starting work I have to do.

Extremely	Moderately		Moderately	Extremely
Uncharacteristic	**Un**characteristic	Neutral	Characteristic	Characteristic

I am continually saying "I'll do it tomorrow."

Extremely	Moderately		Moderately	Extremely
Uncharacteristic	**Un**characteristic	Neutral	Characteristic	Characteristic

Among WTF testers, 86 percent said that the statement "I generally delay before starting work I have to do" was moderately or extremely characteristic of their behavior. And 42 percent of testers said that yep, continually putting things off until the next day is moderately or extremely characteristic of their choices as well. Go online to www.generationwtf.com to take the full test and see how your score compares with others.

Studies from the 1970s have found that three-quarters of college students in your parents' generation procrastinated on their schoolwork. And according to 43Things.com, an online goal-setting community where people can enter in their goals and see what other people are trying to accomplish as well, the number one goal is weight loss. And the number two goal? To stop procrastinating.

In researching this book, I asked hundreds of young adults what they'd most like to get advice about. Common questions included "How can I make myself stop procrastinating?" and "How can I reduce the stress in my life?" The two go hand in hand: By limiting your procrastination, you can take better control of your time and reduce unnecessary stress in your life.

Meet Mr. Procrastination and Ms. Stress

Think of Procrastination and Stress as two people in a dysfunctional relationship.

Procrastination: "Hey, just relax, we'll do it later."

Stress: "I'm worried I won't do a good job on the assignment if we leave it to the last minute . . ."

Procrastination: "If we do it now, it could suck even worse—and then we'll be left with a bad result that we actually tried hard on, which is way more embarrassing."

Stress: "But I'm not having fun doing anything else because I'm getting panicky and anxious that it's never going to get done."

Procrastination: "Simmer down. Maybe something will come along and bail us out."

Stress: "You can't talk me out of my feelings!"

Procrastination—the decision to put off until tomorrow what should be done today—and stress—the frazzled and panicked feeling you know all too well—feed off each other. And in this unhealthy relationship, the usual "just do it" talk doesn't quite cut it.

But all hope is not lost: Good time-management practices, including lots of reminders and checkups along the way, can reduce stress and procrastination at the same time.

People who put an assignment in their planner or calendar immediately, scheduling a time to do it and noting the deadlines necessary to accomplish it, are the ones who are most likely to actually accomplish the goal on time. Smartphones make this easier than ever. (Think of how much time you spend texting—you could make entries in an electronic planner in a fraction of the time.)

If you are a chronic procrastinator (or scored higher than a nine on the procrastination survey at www.generationwtf.com) you'll find resources in this chapter and online that will help you stay on track to achieve your goals.

Why Am I So Stressed Out?

Stress is when you feel overloaded, like everything is too much for you. It's when you'd prefer to pull the covers over your head and not get out of bed for a week—or when you want to scream and cry and throw things out of pure frustration.

Stress can also be a panicked feeling when we're in real danger—but in the modern world, most of our stress comes from non-life-threatening situations. You've got a big deadline coming up. You're having problems in your relationships. You're on the brink of a big life change. Sound familiar? That just about perfectly describes everyday life for many Generation WTFers.

We've all been there. So what can we do about it?

Daily exercise and relaxation techniques like meditation or prayer, and cutting down on the caffeine-alcohol upper/downer combo that gets a lot of us through the day are good starts. But since you're a busy person, learning to manage your time efficiently—and stop procrastinating—can not only help relieve the stress, it can keep it from coming back.

What Is Procrastination?

Procrastination is delaying something that you should do now, and pushing it off for later. It isn't totally illogical behavior. Some people say they do their best work at the last minute. Others say there's no point in worrying about a task until you have to. Still more savvy dawdlers would argue that delaying completion of a project allows all the information to come in before they draw conclusions.

And to some extent, research has found this to be true: In a study of college students, procrastinators seemed to be less stressed out at the beginning of the term than nonprocrastinators. Some forms of stress can actually increase performance. And if you're in a learning environment, it is possible that new information will reshape your approach to a particular assignment.

However, procrastination has also been linked to depression, low self-esteem, anxiety, and stress. In study after study, researchers find that procrastinators are less likely to follow through on an assignment at all and more likely to turn in subpar work.

Waiting until the last minute to do something can work—but only if everything else goes perfectly. Without a buffer of some extra time, you're more likely to miss the deadline when your computer acts up or the bus is late or a chatty coworker pops into your office for a thirty-minute monologue. And that leads to more stress in the long run.

A Little Extra Warning: WTFers are great at rationalizing their behavior as not really procrastinating—when deep down you know it is. Tread carefully when you say to yourself, "It's okay, I've got plenty of time and I won't procrastinate at all tomorrow, so I probably don't have to do any work on it today . . ." Studies show that the overoptimistic

Q   I find it impossible to plan for the future and find myself thinking about the very moment/second I am in. Because nothing else truly exists. Time is a made-up concept, and the future is too ambiguous. —Stacey

A   Spoken like a true philosopher—and a chronic procrastinator, I'd imagine. You're right: The future isn't predictable, and in that sense, procrastination isn't totally illogical. Delaying work on a project might enable you to get more information about how to do it well. The project might become unnecessary. The world could end or you could get hit by a bus.

But this is a fatalistic attitude, and not one that leads to a particularly happy or successful outlook on life, psychologists find. Thinking about why you have this fatalistic attitude is a good first step: Are you afraid of failure? Are you grumpy because other people seem to be bossing you around? Maybe you're just bored with your current job and need to rethink your purpose. But being fatalistic about your life isn't going to help you succeed in the long run.

belief that you won't procrastinate in the future makes it *more likely* that you procrastinate now.

Why Do People Procrastinate?

Some very smart people have devoted their entire professional careers to studying procrastination. Indeed, there's even a Procrastination Research Group at Carleton University in Canada. And while there are many reasons why people procrastinate, among the top three are:

▶ We think we might not do a good job.

▶ It's boring or an un-fun task.

▶ We don't like to feel like we're being ordered around.

Most self-help literature focuses on the first one, arguing that we are afraid of failure and put things off to make sure we handicap ourselves in case we don't do a very good job. This can be a real issue—but psychologists have found that it's the other two that are the biggest culprits: Our emotional reaction to the task guides whether we do it now or later.

Procrastinating on Un-Fun Tasks

When you are faced with a boring, routine task, you're much more likely to push it off until later. Making the bed, filing old paperwork, and doing expense reports are prime examples. It's not glamorous work, but it has to be done. Does it need to be done right this instant? Usually not, so we can easily push it off until later.

But then a friend unexpectedly stops by, and you're apologizing for your unmade bed. April 14 rolls around and you're scrambling to get through all your old receipts to make the necessary deductions on your taxes. Your procrastination catches up with you, and you're stressed out once more.

Solutions

Give yourself a gold-star incentive: Reward yourself in a small way for doing a routine task on time.

Do a quick cost-benefit analysis: Think of how long the task will take, and whether you can break it down into smaller steps. Then think about how many minutes you'll spend stressing over whether or not it's

The Buddy System to the Rescue

WTFers told me that telling their friends and family about their goals (see page 56) was crucial in fending off procrastination urges. "My friends provided accountability—and gave me a reason to follow through with my goals," said Molly. "This is something that I will try to experiment with some more in order to improve that area of my life."

Ashley said she told her boyfriend, friends, and parents about her attempts to refocus and stop procrastinating, and with their support—particularly the support of her boyfriend—Ashley reported that she'd been very successful. "My boyfriend has noticed [that I'm not procrastinating as much] and has been really encouraging about reminding me to tackle what is difficult first. I declined an invitation to go to a movie in order to finish some work I had been previously putting off. I stayed home, got it done, and went to a movie the next night. He was surprised and commended me on following through and it was a really good feeling to know that if someone else was noticing, I must be doing something right. It is also nice to have someone to be accountable to; he serves as a 'check' on progress," she said.

done. We often expend a lot more time worrying about the unfinished boring task than we would actually doing it. So get it over with!

Procrastinating on Tasks That Someone Else Assigned to You

You hate being told what to do. We all do, in fact—and that's only natural. We like to figure things out for ourselves, to chart our own path. That mix of guidance and coddling is what your parents did for so long, and now that you're an adult you want to do it your way, without someone else telling you what to do.

That's fine, say self-help books on individualism and goal-setting going back hundreds of years. It's admirable, really. "Self-help is at the root of all genuine growth in the individual," writes Samuel Smiles in his 1850 bestseller *Self-Help*. By relying on other people to do things for us, we end up "comparatively helpless."

But before you can take charge and plot your own course, you've got to prove to others that you are up to the task. Achieving success on your own is the fastest way to get the world to back off and stop telling you what to do.

Solutions

Think opportunities: If you do this boring task—and do it well— what might you get in return? Acknowledgment from your boss? A chance at a job interview? Reframing the task from one that is being demanded of you to one in which you take ownership can make a big difference.

Think long-term: Remember your core values: How might this task help you accomplish one of those? This can also serve as a reality check, because if the task is one that goes against your core values, it's something that you should refuse, not just drag your feet on.

The Epic Battle of Procrastination vs. Self-Control

You know that image of a devil on one shoulder and an angel on the other, giving you conflicting advice, battling for your soul? Well, think of this as a similar battle—except that for most Generation WTFers, it's not really a fair fight. Right now, Procrastination is beating the snot out of Self-Control.

Fortunately, just like any prizefighter, Self-Control can be bulked up with some daily exercise. And then you've got a better chance of winning the match.

Social psychologist Roy Baumeister finds that "each person's capacity for self-regulation appears to be a limited resource, which is renewable over time and can be increased or decreased as a result of gradual developments or practice." Translation: You can overcome procrastination by building up your self-control like a muscle, slow and steady.

If you're building a muscle, you don't start with the big-boy weights right off the bat. You start small and work your way up. As you get stronger, you see results, and you're encouraged to continue toward your goal. Commitments and rewards in other elements of life work the same way: Start with something manageable, achieve it, and reward yourself along the way.

So, set five commitments—with clear deadlines—and clear rewards. They can be simple: Go to the gym every day for the next week. And if you do, you get to have your favorite dessert. Make a to-do list before you leave the office to help organize the next day's schedule. If you do that for a week, go to a movie on Saturday. Call your ailing aunt—by Wednesday. Buy plane tickets to visit your parents—before the twenty-one-day window closes on Friday and the prices go up. You get the idea.

Commitment _____

→ Deadline _____

→ Reward _____

Commitment _____

→ Deadline _____

→ Reward _____

Commitment _____

→ Deadline _____

→ Reward _____

Commitment _____

→ Deadline _____

→ Reward _____

The Gold-Star To-Do List

In a sense, this is a glorified to-do list. What's different here, though, is that you're not only listing what you've got to do, you're setting a clear deadline and offering yourself a clear reward. In Gretchen Rubin's terrific book, *The Happiness Project*, she writes about how important it is to give ourselves our own rewards, our own gold stars. When you're in school, you get grades and have a shot at achieving various levels of academic honors. In the real world, those accolades are fewer and farther between.

Without gold stars on offer from others, all of our commitments and efforts can seem somewhat pointless. But part of being an adult is giving yourself your own gold star. Little rewards make life a lot better.

Having Problems Getting Started?

In his book *59 Seconds* psychologist Richard Wiseman suggests a very basic technique to help chronic procrastinators get back on track: Just do a little bit right now—and let your nagging brain motivate you to finish the rest.

If it's Monday, and there's a project that's due on Friday, instead of putting off all the work until Thursday night, try doing just a few minutes on it right now. As the saying goes, "once begun is half done." Just do a few minutes of work—brainstorm a bit, outline what you want to say, write a small section or do a short computation.

Research supports this idea—and Generation WTFers who tried this had a lot of success. Mary said, "I experienced a nagging feeling in my head of incompletion if I started a task partially rather than procrastinating and putting it off completely toward the end. In turn, the nagging feelings produced anxiety for me, which almost forced me to dive back in and fully complete what I'd started. Although I felt a slight annoyance due to the 'forced' aspect of it, it actually proved to be remarkably effective."

Josh said, "The true genius of this is that whether or not you finish the task right then and there or your procrastinating side wins and you decided you'll do it later, you've already done at least a modest amount

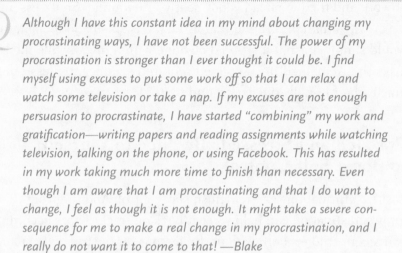

Q *Although I have this constant idea in my mind about changing my procrastinating ways, I have not been successful. The power of my procrastination is stronger than I ever thought it could be. I find myself using excuses to put some work off so that I can relax and watch some television or take a nap. If my excuses are not enough persuasion to procrastinate, I have started "combining" my work and gratification—writing papers and reading assignments while watching television, talking on the phone, or using Facebook. This has resulted in my work taking much more time to finish than necessary. Even though I am aware that I am procrastinating and that I do want to change, I feel as though it is not enough. It might take a severe consequence for me to make a real change in my procrastination, and I really do not want it to come to that! —Blake*

A How do you eat a piece of cake?

Do you eat the frosting first—going straight for that sugary goodness—or do you eat the cake itself, saving the frosting to enjoy at the end? My bet is that you'd go straight for the frosting, and therein lies the problem.

In his bestselling advice book, *The Road Less Traveled*, M. Scott Peck writes that how we eat our cake tells us a lot of about how we approach life. When you were a kid, your parents probably made you do your homework (the cake) before watching TV (the frosting). In psychological lingo, this is called learning to delay gratification—putting off the fun stuff until after some work is done—and it is considered one of the keys to life success.

It's a real-world adult skill that this book can help you learn. Get serious about setting goals in chapter 3 and self-control in chapter 4—and see what tips might work best with your personality.

of work and the job ahead is not nearly as daunting. So it's essentially a win-win situation. I found that if the job is small and menial, then I would simply finish it just so I'd be done with it, meanwhile the larger tasks that remained uncompleted required significantly less effort to finish when I finally did get around to it."

Frazzled and Stressed? Be Nice to Yourself to Boost Self-Control

Positive affirmations can replenish self-control. And forgiving yourself for procrastination can help you get back on track. That's according to two recent studies, both with useful lessons for the frazzled of Generation WTF.

The first study asked participants to write a short essay about something that was important to them—their core values, their relationships, and so on. But half of the participants had to write this essay without using the letters *a* and *n* while the other half could use the entire alphabet. This was a test of self-control: The ones who could write using the whole alphabet used less self-control during the exercise than the ones who couldn't use the letters *a* and *n*.

Then, the researchers asked the participants to submerge their hands in a bucket of ice water. Guess who could hold their hands in the water longer? Those who hadn't had to previously exert self-control.

But here's where it gets interesting: Among the group that had exerted self-control in their missing-letters essay writing, some were instructed to take a quick break afterward and reaffirm good things about themselves—thinking about what makes them proud, focusing on the positives. For those folks, their self-control recovered quickly and they were able to hold their hands in ice water for longer than those who didn't reaffirm positive things about themselves after a trying test of control.

Bottom Line: If you are exerting self-control, you can replenish your reserves by thinking about positives in your life. That will give you the energy you need to tackle the next self-control project in your life with verve.

The second study asked college students to complete surveys about procrastination and self-forgiveness before two in-class exams. The idea was to see whether beating yourself up about procrastinating hurt your exam grades. It turns out that those who forgave themselves for their procrastination leading up to the first exam were less likely to procrastinate when studying for the second exam.

Bottom Line: If you are a big-time procrastinator, don't beat yourself up about it too much. Just make an effort to do better in the future, set clear goals, and make small steps toward achieving them.

A few more tips:

▶ Spend a few minutes every day thinking about the good things and the things for which you are grateful. This can give you the strength to carry on.

▶ Next time you start procrastinating—either in your work life or personal life—think about the things that are important to you. Think about the things that make you proud. Try the gratitude diary exercise in chapter 2 again. Give yourself a pat on the back for all the good stuff you're doing. Remind yourself of your values and purpose.

▶ If you procrastinate anyway, forgive yourself. By cutting yourself some slack for dragging your heels on one assignment, you may have more willpower to work earlier on the next one.

Make a commitment to doing better next time and avoiding the regrets.

▶ These may sound like hokey bits of advice, but if these experiments are on target, you just built up Self-Control to outfight Procrastination in the next battle . . . without breaking a sweat. Give it a try.

Urgent vs. Important: Stephen Covey on Overcoming Procrastination

In his book *The 7 Habits of Highly Effective People*, Stephen Covey offers dozens of guidelines for prioritizing commitments and obligations that Generation WTFers found useful in their own lives. Creating weekly and daily schedules helped them get out of perpetual crisis mode and focus on important career and life ambitions. But to do this most effectively, Covey recommends making a big-picture plan, setting goals, and prioritizing.

It was this three-part advice that WTFers embraced as a winning strategy for getting back on track.

Make a Plan

Your to-do list should include not just the urgent things—what has to be done—but should also include the things you want to accomplish—those important career and personal objectives that often get lost in our frantic day-to-day life. That way, you clearly see the *purpose* for your work: It's not just about doing tasks for someone else, it's about pushing the ball forward to achieve your larger dreams.

Sam said she had previously made to-do lists that "usually contain

Overcome the Old Forces of Gravity in Your Life

Breaking old habits is like overcoming the force of gravity, argues Stephen Covey in *The 7 Habits of Highly Effective People*. And procrastination is a tough habit to kick. Just as astronauts use most of the energy of their spacecraft to break through the gravitational pull of the earth, so too does it take a lot of energy for our "lift off" in breaking habits of procrastination, impatience, criticalness, or selfishness. But once we break through, Covey says, "our freedom takes on a whole new dimension."

One way to supercharge your liftoff: Remember what you want folks to say about you at your funeral. Those core values you hold are the reason are the best motivator to stop dragging your feet on whatever important project you're putting off.

"For most of my life I have been a procrastinator," Chris admitted, but after trying these strategies, he purchased a planner. Whenever he wanted to ignore his responsibilities, he said he thought back to the mental image of his funeral. "That helped me to persevere and get my work done before pursuing other endeavors," he said.

what has to be done, not what should be done." At Covey's suggestion, she added longer-term to-dos to her planner lists. "Looking at future assignments in my classes and fitting their work into each day . . . actually helped a great deal. I no longer felt stressed about exams or papers because I had done a little throughout each week so when it came time for the due date I was more than ready. Every college student says they are going to work on procrastination; however, it wasn't until I put this book's advice into action that I actually stopped putting things off until the last minute."

Just writing things down helped Generation WTFers focus. "You have to prioritize and maintain a good outlook on the future goals if you are to accomplish anything and accomplish it well," said Liz. "I've begun writing down and making to-do lists which has helped to see everything that needs to get done. Everything from appointments to meetings, work times to due dates is written down so it becomes very easy to see what needs my attention first and also plan to do the rest as time goes on."

Set Your Goals

If you skipped that chapter on goal-setting, now is a good time to go back and take it seriously. By setting goals about which you are passionate, you're much more likely to stay on track.

Josh picked two goals he had had for some time now—to buy a new LCD television, and to bench-press 205 pounds—and he applied this three-part strategy of making a plan, setting goals, and prioritizing. He'd just begun saving for the television, collecting all his loose change and putting it into the bank, when he heard that a neighbor was moving and was selling his older TV for $200.

"This television was fairly large and was a good deal at the price. However, if I got this television it would have to come out of my LCD fund. My neighbor's television would be out of date in a couple of years, but I could buy it right now. On the other hand, if I was patient and waited I could have a television that would last longer and therefore be a better use of my money. So I used my self-help advice and focused on my long-term goal instead of being distracted by a short-term one."

At the start of the year, Josh reported he could bench-press "only"

150 pounds, and while he'd been working toward 205 pounds for some time now, he wanted this to be the year he succeeded. After lifting for three days a week all year, Josh was ready to "test out" his "max on the bench" when some friends asked him to play basketball a few times. He accepted and skipped the gym that week. The next week he tried but missed the mark. That's when he began to put first things first to achieve his goal.

"This past month I decided I was going to keep to my lifting schedule and bench 205. I kept to my lifting schedule the first week, and the second week I was ready to test my max. I accomplished my goal and benched 205. I believe that this advice helped me because I wasn't going to let anything else get in my way this time and the advice helped me be more determined in sticking to it. I think that my greatest benefit from this advice is that I now know that I can stick to my goals and I don't have to give up on them."

Josh was pleased with his success and said he would advise others reading Covey's book to "go into challenges with an open mind." He was initially very skeptical that any advice would inspire him and said he wishes he'd "gone in with more of an open mind. I may have learned more and possibly gotten even more out of it. I felt that this self-help advice really made a big impact on me, and that this book did most of the work in inspiring change and I just followed the book's advice."

Prioritize

Putting first things first isn't about rote schedules and to-do lists, it's about priorities. Endless lists can be stressful, as many Generation WTFers reported, but prioritizing weekly goals offered better focus.

If This Sounds Like You, Give the Advice in This Chapter a Try

"As a child my parents would always tell me that I wasn't allowed to watch TV or go out with friends until my homework was done and then all of my daily chores. Even though my parents did their best to help me I still took advantage of the half hour I had until my dad would get home. I was at school all day, why on earth would I want to come right home and do more schoolwork? I progressively got better at procrastinating and finding time here and there to do school work at school only.

"By my senior year of high school I was able to not bring a single piece of homework home the entire school year and pulled a 3.3 GPA. After years of practicing I found it much easier to do as much as I needed to get by and no more. As the years went by I found it just as easy to slide by in college as well. To be quite honest I wrote nearly all of my papers in every class I had the day they were due. In fact I was proud of myself for pulling good grades on four-page papers I wrote in an hour.

→

Liam said the need to prioritize important things—like finding a job—over urgent distractions—like responding to an incoming text message—was a good reminder to have his senior year of college. "I remember a time when I was working on my resume while searching for jobs when I received a slew of text messages from several friends," Liam said. "The text messages, in this scenario, were 'urgent,' whereas my job search was 'important.' Although I considered myself a self-controlled person, before reading *The 7 Habits* I may have answered all of the text messages."

←

"After reading *The 7 Habits of Highly Effective People*, I decided that I would try to implement his advice of putting first things first by writing down all the things that needed to be done and when they needed to be done—and putting the things that needed done first on top. I then went to my planner and wrote in things like 'paper due' on the calendar I always looked at in my planner so there was no way I couldn't see it.

"I also found a Post-It note gadget that I could put on my desktop with Windows Vista. On that Post-It, that I see every time I look at my desktop, I wrote all the things that need to get done. As I finish up things on my list I delete them and the next most important thing is moved to the top of the list.

"I am a type of person that if I don't see it, I don't think it needs to get it done. This advice has helped me to become more efficient with my time and getting things done on time, not because I have never heard of this advice before, but because I forgot about these techniques and how well they have worked for me before."
—Stephanie

Breaking the Procrastination and Stress Cycle

There are tons of other reasons why you might be stressed out . . . and better time management isn't always going to help. But it can come to the rescue in some common stressful situations:

You're balancing school, work, and a personal life? Figuring out your priorities and managing your time as best you can will reduce unnecessary stress.

Looking for a job? Knowing that you've sent out resumes on time, to the right people—rather than procrastinating in hopes that a job will land in your lap—will not only make you less stressed about the process, it will increase your chances of success.

You want to lose fifteen pounds before your high school reunion? Even the worst of the crash diets won't get you there unless you start early. Planning ahead—and rewarding yourself along the way for every small victory—will increase the likelihood that you'll be svelte enough to handle the cattiest of old "friends."

WTF Did I Just Learn?

Congratulations! You passed the second stage of the WTF transformation. If you set some SMARTER goals, if you reviewed the tricks of self-control, if you're ready to take some steps to win the battle against procrastination and stress and if you're excited to apply this knowledge to your life . . . *you just got Tenacious!*

Here's a quick review:

SMARTER goals. Goals give us a direction and focus for our energies. Setting out to achieve goals the SMARTER way (by making them **S**pecific, **M**easurable, **A**nticipating success, **R**ecording your ideas, **T**racking your progress, **E**xplaining to others what you're up to, and **R**ewarding yourself along the way) will help you get motivated.

Self-control. Self-control is learning how to balance the work and play of life. It's about using the ups and downs to your advantage, rather than having them use you. It's about making smart choices that prioritize your future, but not beating yourself up too much when things go awry. As the quip goes, "everything in moderation, including moderation."

Procrastination and stress cycle. Procrastination has been linked to depression, low self-esteem, anxiety . . . and, yes, stress. Yet still, we are all tempted to put off boring or daunting tasks. By tackling a project for just a few minutes, prioritizing urgent versus important aspects of your to-do list, and thinking in terms of long-term reward, you can shatter the procrastination/stress cycle and start relaxing—not dreading your work.

Questions to ask yourself:

► *What are my goals?* What do I want to achieve?
► How can I *break down my goals* into more measurable—and manageable—steps?
► Who can I tell about my goals—and *who will help me achieve them?*
► *How can I be more proactive* in my conversations, and in my life?
► What are some "bright lines" I can create to *steer myself away from temptation?*
► Do I procrastinate too much? If so, *which of the tips in chapter 5 will I try first?*
► How can I *better prioritize my schedule to reduce stress* while focusing on important elements of my future?
► *Have I really committed to a goal?*

If you haven't committed to achieving at least one goal with the SMARTER methods, go back to page 58 and give it a try: *Only you can give yourself a gold star for being Tenacious.*

part iii

GET FEARLESS

chapter 6

Thrift

Old Word, New Secret to Success

HOW DO I PROPERLY PREPARE FOR THE FINANCES, BUDGETING,
AND RETIREMENT ISSUES OF BEING IN "THE REAL WORLD"?
AT COLLEGE, YOU GET AN EDUCATION BUT NO ADVICE ON HOW TO
SAVE MONEY OR CREATE A BUDGET SO YOU CAN LIVE HAPPILY YOUR
ENTIRE LIFE WITHOUT FINANCIAL CONSTRAINTS. A LOT OF PEOPLE SAY,
"START YOUNG" WHEN IT COMES TO SAVING MONEY, BUT HOW
SHOULD WE SAVE IT? HOW DO WE KNOW HOW MUCH TO SAVE, ETC.?
—KYLE

This chapter is your guide to understanding the lost virtue of thrift—creating a good relationship with money that will keep you in the black for decades to come. Indeed, understanding thrift and getting your financial life in order is the first step to becoming a **FEARLESS** you.

So let's see how you think about money and things. On the next page is one of the most popular psychological scales to test this, so let's see where you fall.

Money and You

For the next eighteen questions, provide the answers in the spaces given according to the scale.

Strongly Disagree	Disagree	Neutral	Agree	Strongly Agree
1	2	3	4	5

[__] 1. I admire people who own expensive homes, cars, and clothes.

[__] 2. Some of the most important achievements in life include acquiring material possessions.

[__] 3. I don't place much emphasis on the amount of material objects people own as a sign of success.

[__] 4. The things I own say a lot about how well I'm doing in life.

[__] 5. I like to own things that impress people.

[__] 6. I don't pay much attention to the material objects other people own.

[__] 7. I usually buy only the things I need.

[__] 8. I try to keep my life simple, as far as possessions are concerned.

[__] 9. The things I own aren't all that important to me.

[__] 10. I enjoy spending money on things that aren't practical.

[__] 11. Buying things gives me a lot of pleasure.

[__] 12. I like a lot of luxury in my life.

[__] 13. I put less emphasis on material things than most people I know.

[__] 14. I have all the things I really need to enjoy life.

[__] 15. My life would be better if I owned certain things I don't have.

[__] 16. I wouldn't be any happier if I owned nicer things.

[__] 17. I'd be happier if I could afford to buy more things.

[__] 18. It sometimes bothers me quite a bit that I can't afford to buy all the things I'd like.

How Materialistic Are You?

Go to www.generationwtf.com to find out your score on this materialism inventory—and compare scores with the Generation WTF community.

Materialistic Much?

Congratulations. You just took the materialism inventory—a scale of how much you value things and material goods as markers of success and happiness. Since this is a real academic survey instrument (rather than the usual fluffy feel-good quiz you see in most self-help books) the scoring is a bit complicated. Not all questions are weighted the same, and some are scored as positives, others as negatives. Head to www.generationwtf.com to let the computer run the numbers for you, and find out how your score breaks down in detail.

▶ Do you judge your success based on your material possessions?
▶ Is the acquisition of goods at the center of your life?
▶ Do you buy things just to have the pleasure of buying them?

You'll get an overall score, plus scores to answer these questions about the centrality of money to your ideas of success and happiness. But even without knowing your exact score, I'll guess that you are pretty materialistic. Most of us are. And because of our love of designer goods and bright, shiny new things, we've got money problems. Lots of them.

Graduating seniors have, on average, $20,000 of student debt and more than $4,000 in credit card debt, a nearly 50 percent increase over the last five years. Generation WTFers bounce checks at higher rates and are less likely to pay off their balances each month, racking up those 14 percent interest rates that keep you in the red. If you're lucky enough not to have those problems, you're likely juggling one—or more—part-time jobs to help pay for books, beer, and beyond.

While young adults have always struggled with money, your generation is particularly clueless about personal finance. Wait, wait, wait . . . before you get angry . . . I'm not blaming you. You're clueless about personal finance because you were never taught the basics of thrift.

First, a Little Background

At the risk of oversimplifying a century of American economic history, think of it this way: You've got the Greatest Generation, raised during the Depression and coming into adulthood during World War II. This generation was fairly frugal because they knew what real want was, but they dreamt of raising their children in a much more stable and prosperous world. Those kids are the Baby Boomers, the optimistic consumers of the American Dream. The Boomers, especially the youngest of the cohort, came of age and embraced a borrow-and-spend mentality rather than the thrifty waste-not-want-not attitude of their parents.

As recently as the early 1980s, Americans saved 12 percent of their income. Then things changed, dramatically: The national savings rate plummeted to nearly nothing, and according to national surveys, 63 percent of Americans admit they don't save enough. Indeed, the United States saves less than nearly every other advanced industrialized nation in the world and the average American household has more than eight thousand dollars in credit card debt. These are the households into which you, Generation WTF, were born and raised.

You're among a generation of young adults raised during a time when the savings rate for households dipped below zero and where credit card debt spiked. Maybe you watched as your parents gambled on state lotteries or were taken for a ride by pay-day loan agencies separating the less savvy (or desperate) from their cash. Maybe you learned some pretty terrible lessons about easy credit as your family accepted promises of no down payments on cars and homes, luring even the wealthiest into spending beyond their means. You were raised to consume—and consume on borrowed money if necessary.

So perhaps it's no surprise that the vast majority of Generation WTFers I surveyed couldn't define the word *thrift*. In class, I prompted them:

You've heard of thrift stores, right?

"So thrift means vintage or used?" one student ventured.

Well, no. Not quite.

In part, this is simply a vocabulary issue. You are aware (if only in theory) of the concepts of moderation in spending, the necessity of saving and the idea that there are better and worse things to spend money on in any given scenario, but the fact that your generation can't define the word *thrift* underscores a larger problem: You haven't been taught the thrift skills you need to be successful adults.

And just thinking about thrift in terms of spending and saving reduces an exciting term to mundane balance sheets. Thrift means good use of money, time, emotions, you name it. The root of the word *thrift* is "thrive," meaning to grow and prosper. Thrift is the virtue of making smart choices and understanding the psychology of decision making. Thrift is about generosity, it's about recycling and conservation to help the planet, and thrift is a learned skill.

The full-on awful recession of 2007–9 gave all of us a wake-up call: Learning about thrift is necessary for success both financially and socially, in early adulthood and beyond. After a review of dozens of thrift advice books—including Suze Orman's books geared toward the "young, fabulous, and broke"—I've boiled it down to three steps that will help you get on track:

1. **Learn** what thrift really means
2. **Understand your money psychology** and avoid some common mistakes
3. **Apply solutions** from the best of self-help and psychology

Step 1: Learn What Thrift Really Means

Thrift is about more than just spending and saving money—it's about your core values and choices that you make surrounding wants and needs. While financial planning guides may focus on building up your savings and cutting down on frivolous spending, underneath it all are assumptions about life values and the morality of what we do with our money.

This morality comes from faith traditions, from socially constructed ideas of what it means to be a good citizen, and from economic structures like capitalism. For Benjamin Franklin, who personified and promoted the idea in his *Poor Richard's Almanac*, among other works, thrift meant working productively, consuming wisely, saving proportionally, and giving generously. Thrift was a mark of good character and civic progress, and necessary for both individual gain and social well-being. Franklin wrote about thrift as industry—diligent work, frugality, and conservation. Idleness and waste were at the opposite ends of the spectrum. "Be industrious and frugal, and you will be rich," wrote Franklin, but "beware of little expenses, a small leak will sink a great ship." And at the core of these aphorisms about thrift was the idea that thrifty living was virtuous living. "Nothing so likely to make a man's fortune as virtue," Franklin said.

Keeping up with that theme was Samuel Smiles, a British self-help author who, in an 1876 book *Thrift*, told readers that thrift is the daughter of Prudence, the sister of Temperance, and the mother of Liberty—an essential character trait for good living. And even in the late nineteenth century, thrift was a virtue few possessed, he said. He described the financial landscape of England at the time as full of suffering not from want of money, but from waste of it.

> In "prosperous times" they spend their gains recklessly, and when adverse times come, they are at once plunged in misery. Money is not used, but abused; and when wage-earning people should be providing against old age, or for the wants of a growing family, they are, in too many cases, feeding folly, dissipation, and vice. Let no one say that this is an exaggerated picture. It is enough to look round in any neighborhood, and see how much is spent and how little is saved; what a large proportion of earnings goes to the beershop, and how little to the savings bank or the benefit society.

Sound familiar? This is a pretty good description of the social climate of the last decade of your life as well.

At various times, thrift has been more or less "cool." In the nineteenth and twentieth centuries there were various thrift campaigns to try to get people to save, and to learn about good use of money as a social virtue. Responsible consumerism was the goal of many of these thrift campaigns. Thrift was defined as wise spending, not just savings. Household economy—how to cook, clean, and shop efficiently—was (and is still, in many places) taught in high school home ec or life skills classes, along with penny-counter exercises and budgeting challenges so students learn what it takes to support a family on a nearly minimum-wage income.

Thrift isn't about being stingy with money. Quite the contrary: It's

The "Wise Use of Money" in Action

"If one could resist the urge to spend money frivolously, on things that only benefit themselves, then they could really eliminate a big burden," Josh mused. At present he didn't think he was putting his money and morality in the right order. "Typically, I will spend my money selfishly and on things I don't really need. If I could stop and think about what I am spending my money on, and what affect it will have on my economic situation, I feel I could make a very positive change for myself. That is why I decided to follow [Smiles's] advice of resisting selfish enjoyments."

For four weeks, Josh attempted to implement advice from Samuel Smiles's book *Thrift*. Josh focused on the idea that there was a "right use of money" and he made it his goal to "get my priorities in line." A few weeks into his experiment, a university bill arrived he couldn't afford. He decided to donate plasma—a painful experience that several WTF testers used as a quick-money source

→

about making smart choices, being generous, and getting FEARLESS about your true values, goals, and purpose in life.

Step 2: Understand Your Money Psychology

I really try to be good about money. I say I won't spend too much when I go to the mall with my friends, but then I get suckered into some great sale. My parents are helping me since my job doesn't pay very much, and every time my dad sees me in a new top or something, he'll comment. I'll tell

←

when they found themselves too deep in the red—and after leaving the clinic with the necessary cash, he "decided it was a good time to go to Buffalo Wild Wings. From there I only had fifteen dollars left. Then, that night I ordered Jimmy Johns at midnight. So when I woke up the next day I only had eight dollars left of my original thirty dollars I needed" to pay the university bill, he reported. "Of course a lightbulb went off and I realized I didn't have the money so I had to beg my parents to transfer money into my account. This was an eye-opening experience for me. After that, I took Smiles's advice more seriously because my parents said they wouldn't do it again." Ever since, Josh reported he'd been on a better track with his finances. "My awareness into my own frivolous spending is better but at times I still find myself drifting back into old habits. However, I still believe that this book was positive and was a big help to me."

him it was 40 percent off or something, and he says, "tell me when it's 100 percent off and then I'm interested." I want to be good about spending, but I feel like I just can't get with this whole thrifty thing. —Kate

Well, Kate, join the club. There are really smart people who devote their professional lives to studying people like you. In his book, *Whatever Happened to Thrift*, business school professor Ronald Wilcox suggests four possible explanations for our spending problems.

We focus on the glitz.

We notice the things we covet more than the things we don't. You're more likely to notice that the girl sitting next to you in class has a designer handbag (because you want it and feel that you can't have it) than the fact that she's wearing Target flip flops. You're more likely to notice the BMWs and Porsches in the parking lot than you are to notice the Toyota Camrys. And the more you continue to notice those higher-end things, the more you tell yourself that to be on par with everyone else, you need to go designer.

→**Generation WTF Solution:** Next time you decide "everyone else has a _____" go to Facebook and look through your fifty closest friends. What percentage of them have the thing you want? You think they all have an iPhone, for example, so when you start listing people to back up your "everyone has it" claim fall into the old confirmation bias trap: You only list those friends who have an iPhone. But if you take a random sample of your friends—even your close friends— you might get a different story. By understanding that "everyone else" *doesn't* have it, you allow yourself to stop focusing on the glitz and save money. Also, instead of always comparing "up"—and thinking of the things you don't have—you might try to compare "down" and be grateful for the many things you've got that most others aren't fortunate enough to have.

We're more optimistic than we should be.

Most of us think we've got more control over the events in our lives than we actually do. From a mental health perspective, this is a good thing (otherwise we'd be really depressed), but from a financial perspective this happy outlook can end up costing us money. For example, repeated research has shown that younger Americans believe their life circumstances will generally improve over time. True to form, the vast majority of Generation WTFers believe that the economy will improve in the next five years. But the problem is that our spending coincides with this sunny disposition, making us less likely to save for a rainy day.

→**Generation WTF Solution:** Do a little worst-case-scenario exercise: What if you can't find a job for six months . . . or a year? Do you have the savings cushion to get you through? What if the economy doesn't improve for five years? Should you really continue to float that credit card debt? You don't have to dwell on these depressing scenarios, but if you aren't liking what you see in your ghost of Christmas future, keep reading for tips on how to save.

We don't understand basic financial facts, like compound interest.

The earlier you start saving, the more money in interest will accrue over time. Saving $100 per month with a 5 percent return starting at twenty-five will give you more than $150,000 by the time you retire at sixty-five. Why? Because the interest compounds—multiplying itself over time. Think about it: You save $1,200 per year and multiply that times the forty years of savings . . . and if there was no compound interest, you'd only get $48,000. But what really happens is that you earn interest on the investment, which gets reinvested to make the pot bigger, and then you get more interest on that bigger pot. You can see how this gets good over time. But if you don't start putting that one hundred dollars away each month until you are fifty, you probably won't get the benefits in time to enjoy them.

→**Generation WTF Solution:** Go online to www.generationwtf .com to find tools for calculating compound interest. You'll pick the amount of money you think you can start saving each month, and see where that gets you down the line. Talk about an incentive to start saving young!

Our "mental accounting" doesn't add up.

In the 1980s an economist named Richard Thaler came up with a theory about how we spend. We play tricks on ourselves to justify our spending: If you've just spent $20,000 on a car, you're more likely to throw in an extra few hundred here and there on the bells and whistles because as a percentage of that huge $20,000 amount, it's nothing. We do the same with sales on clothing—spending more than we normally would because we figure it's all on sale so it's "practically free." And the more we trick (or lie) to ourselves about money, the less thrifty we become.

→**Generation WTF Solution:** Think of what *else* you could be doing with that extra money. Next time you are buying an expensive gadget, pause before throwing in the swanky carrying case. If that case costs thirty dollars, think of what else you could do with that thirty dollars. What would it buy you—a night out with friends, perhaps? Then compare those things. Would you rather have fun with your friends or a tricked-out carrying case?

According to some commentators, the upside to the economic slide could be relearning what we already knew: that the party would end at some point and that behavioral change in the form of thrift is necessary for long-term prosperity. To get on track, people in their twenties

---

The Psychology of Money

Don't break the seal. You know the crass saying about not "breaking the seal" when you're drinking—because you'll be going to the bathroom all night long after that? Well, research shows that it's actually true with spending: Buying one thing—even one small thing—tends to open the floodgates for more purchases.

Comparisons are tricky. When we are comparing the purchase of a TV, we look at the price of the Panasonic versus the Toshiba versus the Sony models, right? And in that scenario, we end up spending more because we think, "Hey, for a few extra bucks, I can get a much nicer TV." But psychologists urge you to think about money globally—as in, "What else could I buy with the difference in the price of TVs?"—and you are less likely to be talked into a more expensive model than you really need.

HALT. Are you hungry, angry, lonely, or tired? Are you anxious, depressed, stressed out? Take a break before spending money on anything to address your real issues. Research finds that emotional spending doesn't make us happier in the long run, and when we're in an emotionally compromised state, we're more likely to be distracted by the shiny new trinkets all around us that whisper "I'll make it all better . . ."

→

←

Good debt vs. bad debt. In our minds, we tend to lump all of our debts together into one big pile of panic. But separating them out is psychologically useful, say financial experts. Good debt is an investment in your future: It's going to create value for you in the long run. Student loans, mortgages, and business loans are usually acceptable debts because they allow you to invest in yourself and your success. Bad debt comes from spending more than you earn and not paying off your credit-card balances at the end of the month. It's "bad" not because of any particular moral judgment about those purchases, but because the extra money you pay to the credit card companies in interest isn't helping you move forward in your life. For WTFers, how you define good debt and bad debt can be a personal choice, so it's important to think about it on your own. Sometimes going into credit card debt for a month is a way of floating yourself—and investing in your future. Other times, it's not. Understanding your values, goals, and personal purpose will be key to figuring out what kind of debt is acceptable for you.

and thirties "need to learn the differences between necessities and discretionary spending," writes *Business Week* reporter Steve Hamm, so financial planners are offering classes specifically geared toward young adults, gradually weaning them off their spending habits one luxury at a time.

Being honest about money—and learning the virtue of thrift—is about more than just spending and saving: It's about your values, your goals, and giving yourself the building blocks to financial freedom. For the Generation WTFers I worked with, learning about thrift was the most valuable of the advice self-help guides could offer: Some 81 percent of testers assigned to the thrift group agreed or strongly agreed that the advice offered in their self-help books "was newly relevant because of the tough economic times."

Below are the six best thrift solutions for your generation's financial woes. Want more details and advice? Check out the resources section at the end of the book.

Step 3: Generation WTF Solutions for Thrifty Living

Generation WTF testers read David Bach's *The Finish Rich Workbook*, Samuel Smiles's *Thrift*, and a smaller group tested our advice from Suze Orman's *The 9 Steps to Financial Freedom* and *The Money Book for the Young, Fabulous and Broke*. Then, they came up with some suggestions of their own. The six most helpful ideas?

1. Know thyself.
2. Track your spending.
3. Declare your independence.
4. Eat smart (at home).
5. Think rich and be generous.
6. Embrace the "experience economy."

1. Know Thyself: Apply Your Core Values to Your Financial Life

The Problem: You've got too much stuff, and yet you buy more and more. Case in point: Back-to-school shopping. One late August Saturday at Target, I watched as parents filled cart after cart with "necessities" for their children's college dorm rooms. "I thought we bought this for you last year," one mother asked as her daughter put a microwave into the cart alongside disposable rugs, lamps, and end tables. "Yeah, but it was so gross at the end of the year, we just threw it out."

Generation WTF Solution: Stop accumulating stuff and start figuring out your values. What is the purpose of money in your life? Are you living the kind of life you want to be living? What are your goals? And how is your spending helping you get there?

Steps to Success

Flip back to chapter 1 and remind yourself of your top five values. Write them below. Then think about what financial goal matches these values.

My core values are	To have the means to achieve them, I need to

Stuck? Here's the list that Ashley made for herself:

My core values are	To have the means to achieve them, I need to
Balance	Cut back my "play money" from $45 to $20 per month by not buying soda, coffee, etc. on the run

Security	Put half my paycheck into savings each month
Happiness	Spend my "play money" on things that make
	me really happy, not necessities
Peace of Mind	Create a logbook of savings and plan repayment
	of loans
Love	Set aside $10 every two weeks to treat my
	boyfriend or roommate to dinner, ice cream,
	or a movie

Facing Financial Fears

Victoria faced her money fears as a first step toward setting her goals: "I'm afraid I won't be able to balance spending and saving over time. I'm afraid I'll always be settling in life, usually getting what I need but not necessarily anything I want. I'm afraid of my future with money because I know very little about how it works. I often feel bad about purchasing things, especially those I don't really need, even if I can afford them," she said. "I think some of these fears come from not knowing how self-sufficient I should be concerning my money right now given my status as a student and my limited income." So she created a personal goal: To learn about money so she could control it, not fear it. And by taping her money goals into her wallet, she stayed on track. Every time she went to pull out cash or a credit card, she'd see her money goals and pause. "Having that there has definitely helped me discern which purchases are necessary like grocery shopping, which are manageable like a new book, and which are unnecessary like a new sundress."

Practical Tips

Tape your core values and financial goals to the mirror in your bathroom or in your bedroom so that you can see it every day. Molly said by doing this, "it reminds me that if I want to live independently I need to save an extra few dollars a day, so I can pay for the apartment to live in after college or be adventurous and go to a new country. Those values should always be on the top of my priority list, every single day. Writing down those priorities encourages me to use my money wisely, so I can live up to them."

Clip a small list of your core values and money goals to your credit card so that each time you reach into your wallet to charge something, you come face-to-face with your values, money goals, and commitments. That extra little pause could save you a lot of money. (Go online to www.generationwtf.com to get a credit card–sized template to customize and print.)

Think about the consumption cues you get on a day-to-day basis: Your friends, family, and work colleagues all give you a sense of what "normal" is for your peer group, and what you should or should not be buying or doing. But those cues don't necessarily add up to your values—so take a few minutes to try to separate the two. What kind of car do you think you should be driving based on your social cues? Okay, now how important is your car to your core values? What kind of clothes should a person of your social status be wearing? Okay, now how important is fashion to those core goals? What kind of shampoo do you think someone like you should have in his or her bathroom? And how important is that to you? It's okay to say that some social cues are important to you—but trying to separate these cues from what *you* actually value in yourself and relationships is a great first step to cutting down unnecessary spending.

Why It Works

Thinking about your values—and writing them down where you will see them—makes it easier to remember them when you are debating whether to buy something or not. Indeed, one student said she felt it was a self-fulfilling prophecy: Writing down your values is a commitment that will shape better choices.

David Bach suggests a similar exercise in his financial bestseller, *The Finish Rich Workbook.* "When you understand what's important to you, it becomes much easier to focus on who you want to *be*, then on what you want to *do*, and, finally, on what 'stuff' you *really* want to have," he writes.

Knowing yourself and your financial values gets back to the core ideas of thrift—that it's not about amassing piles of money, but rather about leading an honest, generous life in relationship to money, and recognizing the core values that guide our lives.

Get Free Peace of Mind

"Having a colorful college experience left me with many enduring, great memories but it has also left me with random debts to energy and cable companies from my five-plus residences that have also proven to be enduring," said Sue. Facing up to her fears, she requested her credit reports and made the first step toward cleaning up her record. "It wasn't that I didn't have the money; I simply didn't want to deal with it or see it in print," she explained. Taking this first step gave her peace of mind.

Where to Get Your Info

The Problem: You don't know much about finances, but you do know you're afraid that you're not going to do the right thing. Do you have good credit (what is credit, anyway?) or are you running on borrowed time? It's time to find out, but you don't know where to go.

The Solution: Knowledge is power, and when it comes to money, a little bit of basic knowledge can do you a ton of good. Do this one quick thing:

Get your credit report. Know your score. It's a favorite refrain for Suze Orman and other financial gurus: Find out your FICO score (the gold standard of credit scores, developed by the Fair Isaac Corporation) that's based on whether you pay your bills on time, your credit card balance compared to your credit limit, the length of your credit history, your recent applications for credit, and your mix of credit cards and loans. You can get your credit reports online from Equifax, Experian, and TransUnion—and you can get one free credit report from each every year. Visit www.generationwtf.com for links to all the major credit bureau websites, and a chart explaining what your score actually *means*.

WTF Does Thrift Have to Do with My Life?

Erin said she feels pulled between responsibilities to her family, her friends, her schoolwork, and her boyfriend, and "money plays a large role in where my attention gets focused. I need money to pay my tuition and to buy books and school supplies. I need money to be able to go out and spend time with my friends. I need money to be able to go home and visit and spend time with my family. I need money to be able to do exciting and new things with my boyfriend.

"I have to admit that I am horrible at balancing how my money is spent. My first priority is paying for the supplies I need for my classes, however, I am lucky enough to have help from my parents for expenses related to school and rent. The expense of going out with my friends on the other hand is completely my responsibility, and no matter how hard I try, I seem to always spend at least twice as much as I plan when I go out." After thinking about her true money values, Erin realized that spending money on friends and entertainment was part of her core value of having fun and experiencing life. "I feel as though this is the time of my life that I am able to have the freedom to go out and have fun with my friends. Because I value that right now, I no longer feel as guilty about spending money on the experiences that I value and feel are an important part of this time in my life."

Armed with this new approach to money values, Erin paid for her friends to join in activities with her on vacation. It had become clear to her that she "would rather be generous with my money in order to allow others to have fun than to hoard my money all for myself."

→

←

Understanding her money values helped teach her why she spends money the way she does. The exercise "also showed me that where I place my values now are not where my values will be in the future when I have a marriage and a family. This has allowed me to feel less stressed and guilt-ridden about spending too much money on things such as clothes, food, and social activities . . . it was important to recognize where my values lie right now in order to better understand how I want my money to be spent."

2. Track Your Spending: Figuring Out Where the Money Goes Is the First Step

I need some serious advice on sticking to a budget. Getting out of college and entering the real world, help in these subjects that doesn't come from parents definitely makes things happen in a more adult and mature way. —Amanda

The Problem: You have no idea where your paycheck goes. You work hard for your money, but by the end of the month, you're maxing out your credit card and begging your parents for just a little bit more dough.

The Solution: Figure out how much money you've got coming in—and going out. Do this on a macro and micro level (monthly and yearly, but also weekly) and you'll get a good sense of where you are financially.

1. **Figure out how much money you've got coming in.** This is usually pretty easy (depressingly easy, often). Go back to chapter 1's money journal exercise to do this in more detail (page 48).

2. **Take the Seven-Day Financial Challenge**, created by David Bach in *The Finish Rich Workbook*. Bach guides readers through worksheets to determine earnings and monthly spending and provides a week of charts for readers to take the "Seven-Day Financial Challenge," in which they record every expenditure and note whether it was "wasted money" or not. That wasted money he calls your "Latté Factor"—those small expenses, like coffee at Starbucks, that add up fast. You can do this, too, regardless of how much you make: Track your spending, down to the penny, for a full week—and figure out where the money goes. You might be surprised what your hidden money-wasters are.

3. **Figure out where your money goes using the WTF-specific worksheet on the following pages.** Gather up all your credit card bills, receipts, bank statements, and ATM slips and fill out this form as best you can.

WTF Does My Money Go?

Clear an afternoon or evening to figure out where your money goes: It'll take some time. Ignore any sections that don't apply to you, but if you think they are going to be upcoming expenses in the next year, it's something worth budgeting in. (For example, if your parents pay your rent now, but once you graduate you'll have to float your own living expenses, that's a big-ticket addition that you'll want to prepare for now.)

EXPENSE	TOTAL PER MONTH	TOTAL PER YEAR
The roof over your head		
Rent or mortgage	$ _____	$ _____
Property insurance	$ _____	$ _____
Utilities		
Gas/electric/oil	$ _____	$ _____
Water	$ _____	$ _____
Other home stuff	$ _____	$ _____
Home maintenance (Condo fees, lawn care, security, etc.)	$ _____	$ _____
Food and various sundries		
Grocery store bills	$ _____	$ _____
Pharmacy bills	$ _____	$ _____
Target or Walmart stuff (toilet paper, plastic wrap, baggies, pens . . . stuff)	$ _____	$ _____
Technology and gadgets		
Mobile phone bill	$ _____	$ _____
Internet bill	$ _____	$ _____
Cable bill	$ _____	$ _____
Home phone bill	$ _____	$ _____
Computer purchase	$ _____	$ _____
Printer/scanner/fax	$ _____	$ _____
Smaller technology gadgets and replacements (Lost your iPod? Dropped your smartphone in the toilet?)	$ _____	$ _____
Music purchases (iTunes etc.)	$ _____	$ _____

EXPENSE	TOTAL PER MONTH	TOTAL PER YEAR
Fun, healthy stuff		
Gym membership	$ _____	$ _____
Sporting events	$ _____	$ _____
Outdoorsy gear	$ _____	$ _____
(rackets, clubs, hiking gear, etc.)		
Fun, less healthy stuff		
Bar tabs	$ _____	$ _____
Liquor store tabs	$ _____	$ _____
Cigarettes	$ _____	$ _____
Restaurant tabs	$ _____	$ _____
Take-out and delivery bills	$ _____	$ _____
Entertainment		
Movie rentals and purchases	$ _____	$ _____
Books	$ _____	$ _____
Movie tickets	$ _____	$ _____
Magazine subscriptions	$ _____	$ _____
Gifts		
Charitable donations	$ _____	$ _____
Holiday gifts	$ _____	$ _____
Birthday gifts	$ _____	$ _____
Wedding gifts	$ _____	$ _____
Baby gifts	$ _____	$ _____
Transportation		
Car payments	$ _____	$ _____
Gas	$ _____	$ _____
Parking	$ _____	$ _____
Tolls	$ _____	$ _____
Bus/train/taxi fares	$ _____	$ _____

EXPENSE	TOTAL PER MONTH	TOTAL PER YEAR
Clothes and personal care		
Clothing	$ _____	$ _____
Shoes	$ _____	$ _____
Accessories (bags, belts, jewelry, etc.)	$ _____	$ _____
Haircuts/color	$ _____	$ _____
Personal care (manicures, massages, etc.)	$ _____	$ _____
Cosmetics	$ _____	$ _____
Grooming stuff (hair gels, face wash, etc.)	$ _____	$ _____
Vacations		
Plane tickets	$ _____	$ _____
Hotel	$ _____	$ _____
Vacation activities	$ _____	$ _____
Restaurants	$ _____	$ _____
Fun stuff	$ _____	$ _____
Cleaning bills		
Laundry	$ _____	$ _____
Dry cleaning	$ _____	$ _____
Maid service	$ _____	$ _____
Loans and fees		
Credit card balances	$ _____	$ _____
Loans from your parents, friends, or others	$ _____	$ _____
Credit card and bank fees	$ _____	$ _____
Professional fees (lawyers, accountants, etc.)	$ _____	$ _____

EXPENSE	TOTAL PER MONTH	TOTAL PER YEAR
Education		
Tuition	$ _____	$ _____
Language classes	$ _____	$ _____
Continuing education classes	$ _____	$ _____
Just in case: Insurance		
Auto/motorcycle insurance	$ _____	$ _____
Health insurance	$ _____	$ _____
Life insurance	$ _____	$ _____
Health care		
Doctor and hospital bills	$ _____	$ _____
Glasses, contacts, etc.	$ _____	$ _____
Mental health visits	$ _____	$ _____
Taxes		
City, state, and federal taxes	$ _____	$ _____
Property taxes	$ _____	$ _____
Social Security taxes	$ _____	$ _____
Other stuff		
_____	$ _____	$ _____
_____	$ _____	$ _____
_____	$ _____	$ _____
_____	$ _____	$ _____
_____	$ _____	$ _____

Now, add up all the totals (Yes, you can count that high).

TOTAL PER MONTH	TOTAL PER YEAR

As you look over this list, does anything jump out at you? Horrified by how much you spend on highlights? Head aching over your entertainment expenses? What can you change? The numbers don't lie, so perhaps it's time to get fearless about making changes.

Why It Works

It goes along with knowing your values. (As Socrates said, "know thyself.") If you know where the money is going, you can decide where to cut back. Just saying "I need to spend less" doesn't do much. We need specifics. Alex said the exercises made him step back from simply "satisfying immediate desires and wants" with needless spending on "small, impulse purchases."

Practical Applications

Go to www.generationwtf.com and print out our wallet-sized daily money tracker. Track your spending for a week. List what your buy, how much you spent, and whether you think the purchase was a good

---

Wasted or Well Spent?

It's up to you what counts as "wasted" money and what doesn't. On the fence? Check back in with your values. Does spending your cash this way help you toward your greater purpose? If so, that's money well spent!

A lot of your purchases cost less than ten dollars, right? Junk food, alcohol, chewing gum, bottled drinks, and "impulse purchases" dominated the list of "wasted money" for Generation WTFers surveyed. And they add up.

→

use of money or "wasted money." Once you fill it out, you can post your spending online to compare it with your peers.

Your list might look something like this:

What I Bought	How Much I Spent	Wasted Money
Coffee and bagel	$4.29	☒
Lunch with friends	$11	☐
Card for Sarah's birthday	$3.01	☐
Gas (because I'm always late and drive)	$22.77	☒
Diet Coke from vending machine	$1.50	☒

3. Declare Your Independence: Pay Your Own Way (as Much as Possible)

The Problem: Your parents are getting cranky about helping you out financially. They may be on a tighter budget themselves. And anyway,

← "I discovered that I spend an average of five to ten dollars a day at gas stations and vending machines alone," said Michele. "This was a major eye-opener for me because I realized that I justify each individual purchase because it doesn't cost very much money, but combined together they add up to a very large amount."

Used Words of Wisdom

Maddie, a WTF tester, reported that because she was being thrifty, she purchased a used copy of *The Finish Rich Workbook*, and said "the most influential things were actually written in ink by the lady who had this before me." The previous reader of the book only made it to page sixty-five, but "what is written at the beginning really puts in perspective for me how important parents are in setting your own financial values."

Here's a WTF glimpse into your parents' generation's attitude toward money: Maddie reported that the previous owner of the workbook, a middle-aged woman, started off strong in the first section stating her goals (planning, treating purchases with respect and value, facing her financial situation truthfully) then her proud accomplishments (quitting alcohol, raising Andrew, losing sixty pounds). "But after that things go downhill," Maddie reported. The woman was more than three hundred dollars in the red each month, but more upsetting to Maddie—whose parents taught her good lessons about thrift—was that this woman said her upbringing had taught her that "Money is fleeting, it comes and goes. No need to budget! Buy what you want when you want and figure it out later! We only like 'nice' things. Designer or expensive is *always* best!"

Said Maddie: "Before I read these books I thought much of the information to be common sense, but something people needed to hear as reinforcement and reminders. After reading some of the values this woman was taught, however, self-help books sometimes change people's lives for the better—if they stick to them."

The Skinny on David Bach and The Finish Rich Workbook

In his bestselling Finish Rich series, financial planner and author David Bach asks readers to first ask themselves some important personal questions: Are you living the kind of life you want to be living? Are your dreams being fulfilled? What are your goals? What are your values? "All financial progress begins with telling the truth," Bach writes in *The Finish Rich Workbook*. While accumulating wealth is great—and clearly the goal of the book—to help the reader along that journey requires some soul-searching. "What is the purpose of money in your life?" he asks readers.

The Finish Rich Workbook, and, indeed, the entire series, preaches a message of financial empowerment. "Change your actions, change your life," promises Bach. "Financial clarity is power." With dozens of fill-in-the-blank exercises where readers can set goals, test their financial knowledge, and brainstorm about their core values, Bach asks readers to create a "purpose-focused" financial plan based on life goals. "While it's absolutely critical to know what you have in dollars and cents, it's equally essential to understand what it will take to create a rich life for you as an individual." Money, he argues, is good for three basic things. Money "allows people to live in a way that defines who they are," it makes it possible to do the things people like to do, and it "enables people to buy stuff." He ranks these values in a stairstep pattern, with the first use for money as the most important—the ability to use money to be the person you want to be. Doing and having, the second and third steps, are less important than making sure you are "being" the best you can be.

Testers applauded the thought-provoking exercises in Bach's book—including his trademarked Value Circle and Latte Factor worksheets—but struggled with the latter parts of the guidebook that focused on more "adult" issues like mortgages and estate planning.

What's the most successful way to pay back student loans before you hit thirty years old? How do I calculate interest and figure out a good schedule? —Angie

Student loans usually count as "good" debt. So don't panic too much. But I salute your commitment to paying off your debts and moving on with your life.

Go to www.generationwtf.com and you'll be directed to a handy calculator to figure out how much you have to pay off each month to erase your debt as soon as possible, and how much interest you'll pay along the way.

Let's say you owe $20,000 in student loans with an interest rate of 5 percent. If you pay $200 per month, in ten years and ten months you'll have paid off your loan (and paid about $6,000 in interest.) Bump it up to $300 a month and you'll be able to get clear of those loans by age 30, and pay about $1,500 less in interest as well. Calculate your own numbers online at www.generationwtf.com.

Use your **WTF Does My Money Go?** worksheet to figure out how much you can afford to pay in student loans, given your salary and basic living expenses. If paying off your loans by thirty is the priority, what other things can you trim from your spending to make the necessary payments?

you're not really psyched about explaining to them why you need to spend fifteen dollars on iTunes songs each month. You want to be independent, but you just don't have the money yet.

The Solution: Start building your financial independence. Consider splitting your rent with roommates and other fairly painless ways to save. Thrift leads to savings, and a financial nest egg leads to independence.

Sweet Independence

"Becoming independent is and was the most rewarding feeling. I have not had to call my parents for any reason regarding money in at least a month and a half. Me becoming more independent has helped my family in this respect, with the state of the economy being what it is, any bit of financial relief I can give to my family is more than appropriate. Plus, since focusing on this area I feel much more connected to my school, and extracurricular activities. . . . I have found that I am much more control over my life than I ever thought I could be at twenty years old." —Thomas

Why It Works

Your parents will reward you for even making an *effort* toward financial independence. Keep yourself in the black, and you'll earn their praise and respect. Plus, someday when you really do need a loan—for your first home, perhaps—they might be more likely to help you out.

Practical Applications

Depending on your financial situation, declaring your independence may take some time. But it's not impossible. Here's how:

The Rent Solution: One big way to become less dependent on your parents is to take your biggest expense—your rent—and split it up with roommates. Matt, who is now a few years out of college and married, said he's kind of horrified by how much money he wasted in rent for so many years.

As a junior and senior in college, he chose not to live in his fraternity house or with several roommates—and moved off campus. "I chose

Q *I've got more than $30,000 in college loans. When I started school, I thought it would be okay because I just assumed I could get a job out of college and pay them off. But now I'm a month past graduation and, yeah, I've got forty resumes out, but nothing's happening. I'm getting a little scared about paying off my loans. —Andrew*

A Graduating from college with debt—and no job? You're not alone: 63 percent of grads coming out of four-year public schools and 72 percent of grads coming out of four-year private colleges were in the red as they donned their black tassels. And only about a quarter of grads in 2010 had jobs lined up by graduation.

For information on when you need to start paying off those loans and what to do if you're not making enough cash to cover the monthly payments one great resource is the National Consumer Law Center's Student Loan Borrower Assistance Project. http://www.studentloanborrowerassistance.org/

Among the top tips, according to *USA Today* money expert Sandra Block:

Understand your grace period. You probably have a six-month grace period before you have to start paying back your federal student loans. But look into it to make sure.

Consider deferment or forbearance. "If you're unemployed, still in school or experiencing economic hardship, you can apply to have payments on your federal student loans deferred for up to three years," Block says.

Find out whether you qualify for the income-based repayment program. If you haven't lined up a job—or even if you have a job, but it doesn't pay much—and it looks like it's going to be a long-term thing, your loans could be reduced. "In most cases, your loan payments won't exceed 10 percent of your total income. After twenty-five years, anything you still owe on the loan will be forgiven," Block says. For more information on how to do this, contact your student loan servicer and then you'll have to provide your tax returns as proof.

Extend your payment term. If you owe more than $30,000, many lenders will allow you to extend the term beyond the standard ten years, thus reducing monthly payments, says Block. But remember: Your interest payments will be higher because you're extending the loan longer.

Trim Your Spending While Still Enjoying Life

Declaring her financial independence was a big attraction for Sue, a just-graduating WTF tester who loved Suze Orman's advice about career and financial planning. After reading *The Money Book for the Young, Fabulous and Broke*, Sue chose a job based on its ability to provide long-term growth opportunities and trimmed her spending to embrace new financial maturity.

Job Search: A life of drudgery and painfully working a job you don't like is not worth extra money, Orman writes. "You can't afford to stay put if you are unhappy."

"It was not the advice I had expected," said Sue. "I applied these suggestions to my life in the past two months when I was deciding on which job offer to accept." Sue turned down a "more glamorous" job for one that she felt had better long-term potential. "I feel that I made the best decision by choosing a company that wanted me to succeed and had great opportunities for personal and professional growth. I know that I will be happy to wake up every morning and go to work. I may not have made the same decision if it wasn't for Suze Orman," she said.

Spending: By "trimming" her spending, Sue said she saved $150 and paid close attention to the section on how best to pay off student loans. Orman doesn't chastise students for their college loans, but rather outlines steps to figure out what debts are worth taking on, and which ones to avoid. "I believe that Suze Orman's financial self-help books really can make a difference and lead to financial freedom. I learned about my 401(K), met with a financial advisor, and acquired my credit score. Even though I did not keep track of everything I purchased, I definitely was able to cut back on spending and ultimately saved myself a lot of money," Sue

→

←

concluded. "After reading *The Money Book for the Young, Fabulous and Broke* and *The 9 Steps to Financial Freedom*, I was able to successfully acquire the knowledge needed to improve my financial independence. I now have the financial know-how that will help me throughout my lifetime."

the 'I'll pay more for my own space' method of living. I lived in a two-bedroom apartment with one roommate. So, getting down to brass tacks here, the rent was $900 and my share was $450." But, he said, had he lived with more people in a larger house, he could have brought his rent down to $225 a month and saved more than $5,000 in his last two years of school.

Scaling Back (Beginner's Version): Once you figure out how much you spend, be honest about how much of that money comes from your parents or other external supports. Then scale back: Tell your parents that you appreciate their support and you'd like to say thank you by doing more on your own. Reduce the help they give you by $300 per month, perhaps. Bonus: You'll feel instantly virtuous and adult, and with some clever planning you won't have to give up that much.

Scaling Back (Advanced Version): Make a promise to yourself that you are going to live on your own financially for six months. Get a part-time job if necessary. Scale back on spending. Tell your parents that you appreciate their support and now you are making changes to become completely financially independent. Wow, will they be impressed.

The Skinny on Suze Orman and The 9 Steps to Financial Freedom

In the spring of 2009 Suze Orman was as hot as she'd ever been. She made *Time* magazine's 100 World's Most Influential list, and her latest book, *Suze Orman's 2009 Action Plan*, a guide to the economic crisis, hit the bestseller list instantly (even with Oprah Winfrey giving away the digital version of the book for free on her website—downloaded more than two million times in one week). Viewership on *The Suze Orman Show* spiked 22 percent between 2008 and 2009. As more and more people turn to her for advice, the personal-finance guru told *Time* magazine, "I'm very, very sorry to say that my business is skyrocketing" because of corporate mismanagement and greed. She doesn't see things improving anytime soon: Orman predicts that millions more jobs will be lost and things won't even begin to look up until 2015.

Suze Orman wasn't born a financial expert. Indeed, like many self-help authors, she begins her books with a rags-to-riches story of unfocused career prospects, personal bankruptcy, and lots of hard work to pull herself back together. Testers read her 1997 bestseller, *The 9 Steps to Financial Freedom*, and her 2005 young adult–focused book, *The Money Book for the Young, Fabulous and Broke*, and essays began flowing in extolling the virtues of Suze Orman's practical and spiritual advice about saving, spending, and the role of money for young adult life.

For Orman, thrift is about learning how to make money work for you and help enhance the good things in life—like friendships, relationships, and family. Being thrifty is closely tied to being generous with charitable donations and honestly assessing what you need to live on. "Suze Orman has done an excellent job at rejuvenating and remarketing the virtue of thrift for my generation," tester Victoria said. "Through my

→

←

experience with *The 9 Steps to Financial Freedom* and *The Money Book for the Young, Fabulous and Broke* I have gained essential knowledge about money and thrift, and I feel more prepared for the financial challenges I may encounter in the future."

The *9 Steps* advice is more focused on the values and virtues associated with thrift than the *Money Book*, which is a practical guide and glossary of financial terms for young adults who need a handbook and dictionary in one. In *The 9 Steps*, Orman incorporates traditional ideas of self-help into modern-day language and concepts. Her advice on consuming wisely, giving generously, and saving proportionally is reminiscent of Benjamin Franklin and she updates the spiritual side of thrift by incorporating trendy Eastern religious ideas, including the "dharma of money" and the importance of reciprocity with the universe. Tim said, "Blending of new and old values is really powerful, and she uses it to create a strong spiritual side to money. . . . She intertwines traditional virtues in a way that connects them all and puts them in contemporary situations."

4. Eat Smart (at Home): Restaurants Are for Socializing

The Problem: You spend a ton of money on pizza, hoagies, and burritos. Sometimes it's takeout or delivery meals, other times it's just grabbing a bite on the way to work or class because there's nothing in your refrigerator. And then you might hit a restaurant before you go out drinking with friends, because it's 9 p.m. and you know you'll be unconscious by midnight if you don't eat something first. Whatever the reason, spending too much money on premade food was a common WTF complaint.

The Solution: Think of restaurants—both the sit-down kind and the take-out/delivery kind—as tools for special evenings out with friends. Having someone else make your food frees you up for socializing and works best for that purpose, not for your three-times-a-day feedings. Learn how to grocery shop like a pro, make your own frozen dinners, and yes . . . yes, you can do it . . . learn to cook.

Why It Works

Once again, you save money without sacrificing on fun. You can eat healthier and spend less money by cooking for yourself—and then you take some of that money you saved and put it toward big dinners out with friends. Think of ordering in food as the absolute last resort: Having a bowl of cereal for dinner is a better idea (both in terms of cost and nutrition).

Practical Applications

Grocery shop like a pro by making a shopping list and being smart at the supermarket.

1. **Make a list.** Channel your inner Rachael Ray and think about what meals you'll need for the week, plan out some menus, and make a shopping list before you head to the store. This doesn't have to be super-gourmet, but just think ahead. Think you'll want pasta on Thursday? Make sure to put the noodles, sauce, and meat or cheese on your list when you go shopping earlier in the week. Need lunches for three days? Put sandwich meat and bread on the list (and check that you have mayo, mustard, pickles, etc., before you leave the house so you don't buy duplicates) so you can brown-bag it.

2. Avoid random purchases. The list will help, but while you're at the store remind yourself that just because something looks interesting doesn't mean you'll actually eat it or use it. Especially when it comes to snacks, this trick will save you money—and calories: If you buy the Double Stuf Oreos, you are much more likely to eat them—all week—than if you don't have them in your cabinet calling your name at midnight.

3. Make your own lunches and frozen dinners. You can make sandwiches a few days in advance, which saves time in the morning

WTF Is Eating Smart?

Mark, a WTF tester, said he now spends less on groceries than he did in college, because he's gotten smarter about his shopping. "Comparing how I shopped then to how I shop now, there is a significant difference. I would say that on average we—my roommate and I—would spend about one hundred dollars a week on groceries, most of which were little-to-no-prep foods or straight junk food. I am now married, have a cat, and my shopping trips for two cost on average about seventy dollars a week, including food and litter for the cat."

How did he cut his bill by more than a third? "The main difference is that we shop smarter now. When in college, it was a walk down the aisles grabbing things we liked and not thinking about it again until checkout. Presently, we ask ourselves questions. Do we need this? Is it on sale? Can it wait until it is? How much is the store-brand version? Now, just because we don't need something doesn't mean I'm not going to buy it ever again, but not every time is the time for snacks and treats."

→

when you are dashing out the door. Recycle supermarket plastic bags as lunch sacks—make your sandwich, wrap it in foil, add a yogurt or granola bar, and put it all in a bag you can grab on your way to the office or class.

For dinners, buy in bulk and make meals you can freeze—like lasagna, made in those mini tinfoil bread pans. Or shrimp bakes that can be frozen in freezer bags. Or veggie and chicken curry, frozen in plastic containers, with the rice on the bottom.

4. Switch to store brand. For most stuff, it really doesn't matter

---

←

Mark said he's also doing a lot more cooking and a lot less ordering in. "I have observed a significant change in my ordered food habits, since college," he said. "It is extremely easy to call the pizza or Chinese food place and have them make your food and then bring it to you. But it is so much more cost-efficient to make the food you have from the grocery store. That is why it was purchased in the first place, right? In college I spent money ordering food, on average, about once a day at about ten dollars. This factors in the times I would splurge and buy food for everyone and the times that food was bought for me. Now, I'm not saying that people shouldn't order food ever, but, if the amount of times food was ordered was reduced by less than half then there would be significant savings:"

Ordering in food seven days per week	Ordering in food four days per week	Savings
$70.00	$40.00	$30.00 per week
		$120.00 per month
		$1,440.00 per year

whether it's name-brand or generic. And according to a retailer's study, 43 percent of customers who switched to generic packaged goods *prefer* them to more expensive brands.

5. Go big on things you use a lot. If you eat a lot of cereal, buy a regular-sized box for your cabinet—and then those big bags of cereal to put somewhere in storage. Refill the smaller box with the contents of the big bag, and save a ton (cereal is *expensive*).

6. Refill your water bottles. Ideally, you carry around a metal or hard-plastic water bottle, but if you buy the disposable kinds at the grocery store, you can still refill them a few times. Saves money and you're being (slightly more) green.

5. Think Rich and Be Generous: You've Got More to Give Than You Think

The Problem: You think you're broke so you can't make charitable donations or give nice gifts to those you love. You'd like to "give back" but you're a college student on a tight budget, and money is something you've got to grasp as tightly as you can.

The Solution: Recognize true wealth—wealth of emotions, experiences, and love. While much of the financial advice out there is about overcoming fears and pressures that come with our modern understanding of spending and saving, thrift is about generosity at the core. The idea isn't to hoard money for later—it's to use it wisely. So get outside your world for a bit and help others.

Why This Works
There's evidence that we feel richer when we give back to others: Psychologists have found that "pro-social spending"—spending on friends

or giving to charity—makes us happier for longer than buying things for ourselves. According to a Harvard study, people who give to charity are 43 percent more likely than people who don't give to say they're very happy people. And the findings don't end there: People who give blood are twice as likely to say they're very happy people as people who don't. People who volunteer are happier. Study after study seems to show that service of any kind boosts happiness because it decreases stress.

Oldies but Goodies: Nineteenth-Century Thrift Advice for Generation WTF

"Some of the finest qualities of human nature are intimately related to the right use of money, such as generosity, honesty, justice, and self-denial; as well as the practical virtues of economy and providence. On the other hand, there are their counterparts of avarice, fraud, injustice, and selfishness, as displayed by the inordinate lovers of gain; and the vices of thoughtlessness, extravagance, and improvidence, on the part of those who misuse and abuse the means entrusted to them."

—Samuel Smiles, 1879

Translation: The right use of money isn't simply about saving, it's about using finances to live a more virtuous and worthwhile life, he argues. According to Smiles, right use of money includes generosity, honesty, and justice in financial dealings. The wrong uses of money include fraud, thoughtlessness, injustice, extravagance, and selfishness. And the best way to make men and women thrifty is to make them wise. Education, he argues, is at the core of thrifty living because we're animals at heart that don't want to provide for tomorrow.

How to Have Honest Conversations with Your Parents about Money

"My father lost his job when I was in junior high school and it changed the way I thought about money drastically," said Kayla, a WTF tester. Before, she'd taken for granted that there would always be ample money, and as a teenager, she remembers feeling confused about how she should change her behavior. Suze Orman writes, "Each of our memories is different, but they all lead us to a similar place, places that are riddled with self-doubt, unworthiness, insecurity, and fear," and Kayla said she agreed.

This fear made her initially value the money she had—and "I didn't simply want to spend each of my paychecks frivolously because I have seen what a short supply can do to a family." But soon, she'd "started to take money for granted again. Perhaps this is because I am in a sort of denial that what happened to my father could ever happen to me, but this incident from the past also explains why there is always a nagging feeling that all of my income could vanish at any moment. Maybe this is why I was so drawn to the entire virtue of thrift, because it resonated so well with my life experiences," she mused.

Kayla used *The 9 Steps to Financial Freedom* advice as a way to start an honest conversation with her parents about finances—something that had before been a taboo subject—and used Orman's online "Action Planner" to remind her of the smaller, yet important, financial literacy tasks.

"I've also been dutifully trying to contribute to my savings account after receiving each paycheck, in order to capitalize on the interest available to me and to avoid letting it all sit in my checking account where I can freely spend it. I'm on track to reach my goal

→

(What we don't know is whether happy people give, or giving people are happy . . . but cover your bases and test it out for yourself.)

Practical Applications

Don't have that much money for a good cause? Volunteer your time. See chapter 8 for more ideas on how to do this.

Don't have cash for a big gift? Say thank you in other ways. Tim wanted to thank his parents for a recent family vacation. So he gave them a small gift card to their favorite restaurant, along with a nice note. "It was a little way of showing my thanks, and it's things like this that I think money really holds value with. It's not about having a lot of money; it's what you do with the money you have, even if it's not a lot. Like the saying goes, it's the thought that counts."

←

amount, and that physical evidence of progress has really been encouraging. However, even though I was able to accomplish some of these smaller tasks, I found it ironic that these were the hardest to check off of my list. I would continually put these more minor details off, thinking that they could happen at any time and that I should focus more on my bigger goals."

While Kayla acknowledged that examining her childhood experiences with money didn't immediately contribute to her bottom line, "it gets to the root of what may be holding them back from that outcome; it forces the reader to confront any issues they may have had with their past or present financial situations and, thus, adds the element of virtue or morality to an otherwise quantified variable."

6. *Embrace the "Experience" Economy: Spending Money on Experiences, Not Things, Makes You Happier*

We all know the saying that money doesn't buy happiness. But it does seem to allow me (or hold me back from) doing fun things with my friends. It takes money to go out to a concert, to go on vacation, to do things. So in that sense, doesn't money buy happiness? —Brandon

Welcome to the experience economy—where the best things on sale are memories. Rather than selling goods or services, for the last few decades, we've been bombarded with experiences for sale: Theme restaurants, amusement parks, vacation packages. Yes, in many ways this is just another sales trick, but it has a really interesting psychological effect: Spending your money on experiences, not things, makes you happier.

Why? Six reasons:

It's easier to compare—and thus be unhappy—with things. It's a lot harder to compare the twenty-five dollars you spent on a concert ticket with any other number of things you could have done with that money because a lot of things happened that night. It all goes as a package and left you with a particular (if not very specific) feeling. But it's a lot easier to compare, and be bummed out by, the choice to spend twenty-five dollars on athletic socks versus a cool new jacket that you saw on sale the next day.

You use a different strategy when buying things. When you buy a pair of jeans, you might try on dozens of them, trying to find one that makes your butt look just so. But you don't spend the same amount of time comparing possible experiences you could have. And that's a good thing. When you try to maximize (i.e., compare all possible options), you tend to be less happy with your choice than when you "satisfice"—picking the first option that seems to fit your criteria.

You second-guess things more than experiences. If you buy the latest gadget, you are constantly thinking about its benefits and drawbacks. If you spend that $600 on a vacation, you are less likely to agonize over the other places you could have gone.

Things go out of style. Memories don't. Your iPad will be considered old news in a year, when a newer version comes out. But the thrill of skydiving with your buddies will be a memory that will always make you smile (or feel queasy).

Prices drop on things—not on experiences. How many times have you bought something one day only to kick yourself when it goes on sale the next? That doesn't tend to happen with our memories of happiness.

A cheaper alternative appears. It's a similar frustration when you find a better—and less expensive—alternative after you've already plunked down your hard-earned cash. But with experiences, you're more likely to say that they were . . . wait for it . . . you knew the joke was coming . . . *priceless.*

WTFers tested these ideas, based on advice from psychologist Richard Wiseman's 59 *Seconds* to spend money on experiences rather than things. And it worked: Investing in experiences gave them a boost that buying things didn't.

In the past, Dennis said he was very much of a things-equal-happiness kind of a guy. "I like playing video games and using my computer and being alone to find happiness. However, it was time for a change. I decided to try to spend more time with my family and rebuild the bond I lost with them as I grew older."

Doug bought concert tickets and noticed that he gained "happiness from the anticipation. For me, concerts are more than a one-night experience. In the weeks leading up to a concert, the added experience of listening to the music and discussing what songs the artist might perform provide the most happiness."

Fight Materialism with Knowledge and Experiences

Thrift means using money in ways that will help you thrive, and in this chapter we've seen that materialism—focusing on things—doesn't buy happiness. What does boost your wellbeing is understanding your financial values, tracking your spending to make sure it's in line with your income and your goals, understanding the psychology of money and spending on experiences—like going out to a restaurant with friends—not things, or unnecessary quick-fix take-out meals.

Only you can commit to being thrifty. Only you can know what money is wasted, and what is well spent. Only you can take the first step to getting fearless. So before you move on to the next chapter, set a time in the next week to get a handle on your finances and fill out the "WTF Does My Money Go?" worksheet.

Today is _____.

After looking at my schedule, I will set aside a few hours on this date _____ **to get fearless, gather my financial information, and figure out WTF my money goes.**

Become a Fearless You

You want to find the right career track—and then land a great job, right?

Maybe you've used this book as a job-search guide all along, clearly laying out your professional values in chapter 1 and identifying your job-search goals in chapter 3. And after facing your finances in the previous chapter, you've taken the first step in becoming Fearless.

Think of this chapter as the finishing touches, a few more of the life skills you need to ace an interview and succeed in the real world—both in your business and personal life. In the lean hiring years in 2009 and 2010, Generation WTF testers tried out a variety of self-help advice and came up with five key bits of advice that helped them succeed.

1. Smile. (Seriously)
2. Admit it when you're wrong.
3. Avoid arguments by thinking win/win.
4. Interview like a pro.
5. Do an honest day's work.

They are all fairly simple—but you'll be surprised by how effective they can be.

Life Skill 1: Smile (Seriously)

A smile is the universal language of welcome, of happiness, of pleasure. Indeed, all humans seem to recognize a smile as a good thing. Before there was any lab-tested proof of the power of a smile, the advice industry had grasped the power of this costless technique. A simple smile was among the top principles Dale Carnegie would teach the young men and women who came to his career and public speaking workshops in the 1930s. Even if you don't feel like smiling, he said in his bestseller *How to Win Friends and Influence People*, force yourself to do it. "Act as if you were already happy, and that will tend to make you happy."

Indeed, research has now proven this: Holding a smile for at least fifteen seconds—even when you feel down—can lift your mood considerably. Yes, we smile when we're happy . . . but the reverse seems to be true as well: When we smile, we become happier.

Dale Carnegie was right: Smiling helps people be happier and nicer to you, too. Try it yourself:

Smile in interviews. Liam was following the advice from *How to Win Friends and Influence People* as he searched for his first job out of college. In interviews, he said, "I would frequently smile and to my surprise it worked wonders. My smiling seemed to induce smiling on behalf of the interviewer, creating a more comfortable setting."

Smile at the office. Sometimes encouraging yourself to put on a smile—even when you're not feeling very perky—can quickly turn into a genuine expression of happiness at the reactions of others. Gina said she felt more "satisfied" at work with her colleagues and even with strangers when she put on a happy face.

Smile when you're walking down the street. "I usually have a

Q *Will my nose ring really keep me from ever getting a job ever, or is my mother full of crap? —Amy*

 A While I'd consider taking it out for interviews, a winning smile will usually get folks on your side pretty fast.

'back-off' face when I'm walking or working alone, my friends tell me. I furrow my brow, focus my eyes downward, hunch my shoulders, and put on what can only be called a scowl. I noticed that when I have this face on, I get very angry with people on the street," said Andrew. After following the advice to smile more often, "it made a big difference: When I held the smile, I laughed a little because I felt silly and unnatural, but I was happy. When walking, I straightened my back and looked up at the skyline and at the trees, and I felt noticeably happier."

Smile when you talk on the phone. A team of researchers at the University of Portsmouth found that people vocally communicate a smile—even when you can't see them. So smiling in phone interviews, chats with your long-distance significant other, or your parents can make the whole world smile with you.

Smile at airline check-in and security personnel. And other people who usually get yelled at by angry customers. Not only is it a nice, kind, and polite thing to do, but you're more likely to sneak an overweight bag onto the plane or get that 3.2-ounce liquid container into your carry-on.

In the next week, I'll commit to smiling a bit more when

As someone who has always just had a small number of close friends at any one time and was fine with that, I have found it difficult lately to small talk with people and develop a network of some sort. It's hard for me to pursue relationships with a large number of people because I'm not very forward. How do I become more personable with people in authority positions, and learn some skills that would help me throughout my life with that? —Jake

 Smile. Show genuine interest in others. Ask questions—and listen to their answers. If you make a person feel valued—and not in a fake way—they are much more likely to continue to want to hang out with you, offer advice, and network. And know that, oftentimes, the other person is just as uncomfortable as you are in that awkward social situation. By taking this approach of showing genuine interest, à la Dale Carnegie, you'll put everyone at ease.

Life Skill 2: Admit It When You're Wrong

"If you are wrong, admit it quickly and emphatically," advises Dale Carnegie in *How to Win Friends and Influence People*. He tells of walking his dog off-leash at a local park, and immediately admitting his error when he saw a police officer approaching, saying he'd been "caught red-handed." Because Carnegie appealed to the officer's sense of importance, and admitted his mistake first, he escaped a fine. "I admitted it quickly, openly and with enthusiasm. The affair terminated graciously in my taking his side and his taking my side."

Sometimes you say the wrong thing. Or you do the wrong thing. Or you offend someone unintentionally or just generally screw up. Admitting you're wrong—before someone else starts really nailing you for being stupid or hurtful—is great on four levels.

▶ First, it's the right thing to do.

▶ Second, it's a lot easier to take criticism from yourself than from someone else.

▶ Third, people are less likely to continue to condemn you if you're already apologetic.

▶ Fourth, especially in a work setting, it makes you look professional and worthy of trust. It shows both your colleagues and superiors that you don't shy away from responsibility or pass the buck.

Nick saved himself a hefty speeding ticket by following this advice. After getting pulled over by a police officer, "I decided to go the same route as Carnegie and appeal to the officer's sense of importance," said Nick. "I kept my cool the whole time, and admitted my fault. I asked to be informed on the location of the speed limit sign, and the area that it covered. . . . Instead of 'breaking lances with him,' as Carnegie calls it, I was able to leave with nothing more than a warning and an experience which will allow me to avoid the same mistake twice." Nick said that it "surprised me on how applicable the advice is. I feel that I have naturally started doing more of what is suggested in the book and have started to see the benefits."

Try it. It's actually quite empowering. And it really takes the wind out of the other person's anger. It's hard to stay mad at someone who is honestly, sincerely apologizing.

Looking back, I probably should have admitted I was wrong when _____

_____.

Looking ahead, a good time for me to admit my mistakes will be with _____

_____

> ## Great Times to Admit You're Wrong
>
> ▸ When your mom calls, angry about [anything and everything]
>
> ▸ When your significant other is hurt that you [did whatever stupid thing you did]
>
> ▸ When your boss finds an error in your work
>
> ▸ When you're late

Life Skill 3: Avoid Arguments by Thinking Win/Win

In game theory, the name for a game with one winner and one loser at the end is called a "zero-sum" game. It's a competitive situation. You can think of it like cutting a pie: A bigger piece for me will mean a smaller piece for you. Fortunately, most of the time, life isn't a zero-sum game—and some of the best advice about interpersonal interactions focuses on how to think in terms of a "win" for everyone.

How to Win Friends and Influence People devotes a chapter to avoiding arguments. But it was Stephen Covey's advice in *The 7 Habits of Highly Effective People* that Generation WTF found most useful: In the fourth of his seven habits, Covey advises readers to have an "abun-

Exaggerate Much?

Josh admitted that, "at times, I find myself stretching the truth. I believe that I got this habit because I have always liked to tell stories, and stories are always more interesting when you add in your own version." So he attempted to follow Carnegie's advice to admit mistakes quickly and emphatically. "Over my lifetime, many people have caught me exaggerating a story but I would usually stretch the truth further and it would escalate from there. However, if I could learn to admit that I was wrong up front, I would alleviate a lot of unnecessary stress in my life," he said at the outset.

A month later, Josh reported that this was "the best advice from a book I have ever gotten." Friends and family were initially skeptical about his chances of success, since Josh had been "telling elaborate stories" since he could talk. But, slowly, he began to speak the truth.

"At the end of the experience, I could honestly say that every time I apologized, I had honestly fudged the truth on accident. My greatest moment of success was when I was telling a story involving my friend and he heard me and said I was telling it wrong. At this point, I would have typically called him a liar, and said that he just wanted to make himself feel cool. However, this time I agreed with him even though I felt he was wrong, and I apologized to him. This felt amazing to me. In some ways, you could say that I made myself look bad, but I felt ten times better for just saying I was sorry and moving on. It saved an argument between me and my friend, and later another of my friends who knew I was right asked me why I didn't argue and I told him he believed he was right so I agreed with him. I feel like this was a big step for me and the rest of the time went over very smoothly as a result. . . . This was a team

→

> ←
>
> effort: The book told me the advice but I still believe a great deal of work was on my end. With any advice you get, a lot of the work is on your end but I am starting to believe that self-help books are more suggestions that you yourself have to take the initiative to make a real change."

dance mentality," recognizing that there are plenty of wins out there for everyone. To be an effective person means looking for win/win situations, seeking a balance of courage and consideration, especially early on in relationships or group work.

To understand the concept of interdependence and the importance of the win/win scenario, Covey asks readers to consider the "emotional bank account" they have with various people in their lives. When you attend to little things, keep commitments, and show personal integrity, you make "deposits" into that emotional account and shore up your relationship. When you break your promises or do something unintentionally hurtful, you make a "withdrawal." The idea is to keep all your emotional bank accounts in the black.

Win/Win with Family

Feeling like your emotional bank account is in the red with family members? Generation WTFers said they tried helping out more around the house when they were home for holidays and that made a big difference. "I offered to cook meals, run errands, or clean something around the house so that my mom wouldn't feel so burdened. Helping her out gave us more time to spend together and her appreciation for my ini-

Generation WTF Praise for How to Win Friends and Influence People

Carnegie conveyed "the importance of truly listening to and considering what others have to say rather than just telling them what you have to say." —Taylor

"Remembering names was great advice—because it actually works and also has negative effects if you don't do it!" —Brittney

"It's very easy to follow; short, specific bullet-points and lots of examples for how to apply the advice in day-to-day life." —John

"My favorite part about his advice is thinking about the other person and how they would feel. Seeing the good in people and being sincere really helped me." —Stephanie

"His advice was geared toward kindness and being positive about others. This will go a long way." —Erin

"His advice made sense, it was down-to-earth and it was easy to apply in everyday life." —Lizzie

"I liked his advice about admitting your mistakes and talking about them first because it's simple to do, but no one ever does it." —Christopher

"I liked the back-to-the-basics ideas about complimenting people and focusing on the good things. It's a positive approach." —Kaelynn

"Finding positives but avoiding arguments when it isn't super important was great advice. It's realistic and healthy for you as a person to use in the real world with others." —Maddie

The 90/10 Rule

The 90/10 Rule—aka the Pick Your Battles Rule—is simple: If you are relaxed about 90 percent of things you're more likely to get your way on the 10 percent of things you really care about. For example, let's say you don't really care where you go to dinner or what movie you see. In those cases, you go with the flow. Then, for the 10 percent of big stuff you do care about, you've got a lot of credibility built up and can more easily draw the line about what works and what doesn't.

Think about how you can apply a 90/10 Rule to your own life. At work? With your close friends? What can you be chill about now so that you're more likely to get what you really care about later? It's not about being a pushover. It's about picking your battles. Everyone wins.

tiative and consideration was well received," said Victoria. "When I'm home I am now much more in tune with creating a more harmonious and balanced relationship. She notices when I offer to run errands for her or cook a meal, and she tells me she appreciates the time we spend together watching movies or shopping or even just conversing."

Win/Win with Friends

Angry at a friend for something? Think of a way you can both be happy. Faye agreed to let a friend borrow her car for a few days, but was livid when she discovered that the car reeked of cigarette smoke when it was returned. "I took my car to the carwash and got my interiors

Ask a Favor, Make a Friend

In *59 Seconds*, psychologist Richard Wiseman encourages readers to take a page out of Ben Franklin's book: To get people to like you, ask them for a small favor. This is the ultimate win/win scenario.

Way back when, Ben Franklin asked a fellow legislator to borrow a hard-to-find book that Franklin knew this other guy had in his library. The man agreed, and after Franklin returned it, the two struck up a conversation—something that they hadn't really done before. "He that has once done you a kindness will be more ready to do you another than he whom you yourself have obliged," Franklin is quoted as having said.

To try the "Franklin Effect," Wiseman encouraged readers to ask people for small favors—as a way to foster a stronger, happier relationship. WTF testers tried this out—and said it works . . . but *only* when you do it face-to-face:

Borrow something. Derek borrowed a video game from a friend who had been "going on about it" for a while. "He perked up immediately and began raving about how awesome the game was. Over the next few days that game became a major point of discussion. . . . I was pleased that I could have a nice interaction with a friend that I hadn't spoken to in a few months."

Ask a favor. After running into an old friend, Lark said she "was rather distant during our conversation, but when I asked a favor of her she was much more friendly and sympathetic. Later on that day I saw her again and I noticed that she was less distant and even hugged me. I hadn't talked to her for a long time, but again we were united by this common goal—I'd simply asked her to watch over my sister since she had some classes with her—and since she also has a younger sibling, I could feel her empathize with me."

Solicit some advice. Mary asked a friend who loves design to offer

→

←

advice on decorating a new apartment. "Not only did she willingly help with my blinds and compliment my choices, but also she then offered to help me with my latest project of producing a photo collage to go up on my wall."

But whatever you do, make your requests in person. Asking for favors via e-mail or text message wasn't nearly as effective as asking (with a smile!) in person, testers said. Ben Franklin wouldn't imagine it any other way.

cleaned. After I cooled down, I spoke with my friend the next day. I asked her if she'd smoked in my car, and when she said yes, I asked her to explain why she thought that was an okay thing to do." Her friend rationalized that since Faye didn't complain when she smoked in front of her, she didn't think it would be a problem. Also, she didn't think a few cigarettes would "stick" in the car. The two were able to think win/win and the friend agreed to pay for the cleaning and not smoke in the car again. In turn Faye agreed to continue lending the car in the future.

The relationship in which I most want to practice this win/win attitude is _____

_____

_____.

I'll begin to embrace my win/win attitude by trying the following

_____

_____.

Life Skill 4: Interview like a Pro

Everyone wants to feel important. And this is especially true when you're interviewing for a job. Obviously you want the company to think you're important enough to hire, but the key to a great interview—and to getting people to like you in general—is to show that you think *they* are important.

Advice books have been preaching this message for decades, but it's a lesson that WTFers found especially helpful: Show employers what you can do for them, show interest in their company, and you'll go a long way toward making yourself their top choice for the job.

The Skinny on Dale Carnegie's How to Win Friends and Influence People

Carnegie tells readers that his book is an "action book," one meant to make an individual successful and well liked. The initial "eight things this book will help you achieve," brands the book as a how-to manual of success and seems to offer unlimited benefits, if only the reader will pay close attention. "Get out of a rut, think new thoughts, acquire new visions, discover ambitions; make friends quickly and easily; increase your popularity; win people to your way of thinking; increase your influence, your prestige, your ability to get things done; handle complaints, avoid arguments, keep your human contacts smooth and pleasant; become a better speaker, a more entertaining conversationalist; arouse enthusiasm among your associates."

To achieve these goals, Carnegie says a reader simply needs "a deep, driving desire to learn, a vigorous determination to increase your ability;

→

←

to deal with people." The book is structured as an interactive workbook; ideas are broken down into points, and then summarized further as bullet points at the end of each chapter. Every section contains a principle, such as "Be a good listener. Encourage others to talk about themselves," which is explained thoroughly in the chapter, and then highlighted again at the end. Repetition is the key to learning these skills, Carnegie suggests. Important quotes—often from Emerson or James—are stated and then restated in italics, all points are made and summarized repeatedly, and the reader is encouraged to make multiple reviews of the book's principles. The final pages of the book are left blank for the reader to write down his thoughts and experiences as he acts out the advice.

The tone of the book is congenial, but not condescending. Carnegie uses "Let's remember that next time we . . ." and other familiar terms, making the reader feel as if he is part of a select club with the advantage of private knowledge. Criticized for its superficiality, *How to Win Friends and Influence People* nonetheless "confirmed as much as it stimulated broad feelings," about how society works, writes social critic Donald Meyer, describing the book as "one of those pulse points in modern American popular culture where the murmurs and racing of hidden currents can be discerned." It was a book about rules for action, not just thought. Readers were advised to read each chapter carefully and then put it into practice, with monthly or daily refresher readings to reinforce the strategies of success.

Dale Carnegie's *How to Win Friends and Influence People* was a number one bestseller during the Great Depression. With a quarter of the working population unemployed at the peak of the Depression, many good people had their life savings wiped out and were desperately seeking employment. Carnegie's advice worked for millions of Americans back then, and Generation WTFers got great results using it in their twenty-first-century interviews.

Liam, a graduating senior, said he applied Carnegie's "six ways to make people like you" during interviews for jobs at Chicago engineering groups. Liam said negotiating with recruiters and potential employers offered plenty of opportunities to test out the advice. In interviews with his eventual employer, he made "a conscious effort to actually care about what the recruiter was saying." It wasn't too difficult, but he was amazed by how well it worked.

"Carnegie's premise that everyone wants to feel important is rock bottom solid, and it is missing from academic psychology."
—Psychologist and professor Martin Seligman

Here's what he did to ace his interview using Carnegie's techniques:

1. Smile. "I would frequently smile and to my surprise it worked wonders. My smiling seemed to induce smiling on behalf of the interviewer, creating a more comfortable setting."

2. Use the interviewer's name. "Remembering that Carnegie says 'a man's name is to him the sweetest word in the English language,' I repeatedly referred to the recruiter by his first name, Scott, which I believe also worked to create a more comfortable atmosphere."

3. Listen carefully. "I employed an active listening technique that Carnegie stresses to improve the relevance of my responses. By listening carefully, I was able to tailor my responses and comments with success."

4. Speak their language. "As I was interviewing with a third-party logistics firm, I made sure to include many industry-specific terms which I could tell greatly impressed the recruiter."

5. Say thank you. "I worked to make the recruiter feel important by deferring to him and thanking him."

Not only did Liam get that job, but he landed several others as well. Carnegie's advice worked because he expressed a "'deep, driving desire to learn' how to deal with people. My implementation was successful, and it helped me to receive a few job offers—a benefit that I greatly cherish, especially in these times."

Are you working on a cover letter or preparing for a job interview? If so, think about what you could offer to the company and jot down some notes here.

The specific goals of the company are:

1. _____ .

2. _____ .

3. _____ .

I can offer my skills of:

1. _____ .

2. _____ .

3. _____ .

By being sure to mention those clearly in your cover letter and interview you will show a future employer that you have researched the organization and that you are ready to contribute to the company goals.

Six Ways to Make People Like You

According to Dale Carnegie's *How to Win Friends and Influence People*, here are the six principles for making people like you. Try this in professional settings to ace a job interview—and in personal settings to make friends fast.

Principle 1
Become genuinely interested in other people.

Principle 2
Smile.

Principle 3
Remember that a person's name is to that person the sweetest and most important sound in any language.

Principle 4
Be a good listener. Encourage others to talk about themselves.

Principle 5
Talk in terms of the other person's interests.

Principle 6
Make the other person feel important—and do it sincerely.

Life Skill 5: Do an Honest Day's Work

It's hard when you see people in the business world cheating all the time. The message that sends to the rest of us is, sure, honesty is great, but success at any cost is better. What are some keys to business success for a young person in their economically downturned world? —*Mike*

Recently, Generation WTF has seen a lot of business corruption— and all the harm it can do. At a time when Ponzi schemes, investor fraud, and high-level deception seem to dominate the news, Generation WTF testers were glad to be reminded of the fact that honesty and hard work are, indeed, the best ways to success. And at the risk of sounding preachy, this is Life Skill 5 because the WTFers I interviewed were passionate about reclaiming business ethics and honesty in the workplace.

The majority of Generation WTF believe it takes hard work to get ahead, according to University of California, Berkeley survey. It's not luck that's going to get you that promotion, say 70 percent of young adult respondents, it's grit and an honest work ethic. So perhaps it's no wonder that the testers who read and applied advice from Samuel Smiles's 1880 book, *Duty*, said it was full of refreshingly old-school reminders that their generation didn't have to follow the same dishonest path many current business leaders seem to be on. Part of being fearless, these WTFers said, was putting in an honest day's work.

It's cowardly to lie about how much work you've done, Smiles told his readers more than a century ago. Deceiving another person is an act of disservice. And sloppy or inauthentic workmanship is dishonest and selfish. Translation: It's cowardly to spend hours on e-mail on company time and then blame a coworker for why your project is late. Be honest at work, and you'll be rewarded.

"If a person does not put forth 100 percent effort and do the best that he/she can, that is considered being dishonest," said Eileen. "I believe Smiles's methods should be implemented more at the workplace because many employees do not always make the best ethical decisions when it comes to business. The importance Smiles places on honesty in his self-help teachings could ultimately benefit many readers," she said.

How do I appeal to employers if my resume isn't the strongest? —Eric

According to CareerBuilder, here are some important things to mention on your resume to catch employers' attention:

- ► Internships
- ► Part-time job (in any area)
- ► Volunteer work
- ► Grades and class work
- ► Military, Peace Corps, or AmeriCorps work

In an interview, try some of the Dale Carnegie techniques that WTF tester Liam used to rock his interviews (on page 197): While experience is crucial, employers also look for someone who is

- ► A good fit with the company culture
- ► Full of good ideas and questions in an interview
- ► Prepared with the proper educational background for the job
- ► Enthusiastic
- ► Knowledgeable about the company

Smiles's advice was "easy to apply," "realistic, practical, and full of obvious guidelines," said WTF testers, and while it didn't "say anything drastically different from what everyone already knows," said Ashley, readers who take Smiles's advice seriously should make a pact to "work harder to acquire an honest days' work, stop lying to themselves and telling others 'little' lies. It is just up to the reader to take the advice and apply it. There are typically very little, if any, external constraints hindering your ability to speak the truth as you know it, to yourself and to others."

"To thine own self be true," wrote Shakespeare. We know that part of

What qualities set a person apart in the new hiring workforce after graduation? —Kristina

Here's a quick tip, à la Dale Carnegie, that worked wonders for WTF testers: In your cover letter, focus on what you can bring to the company or organization rather than telling them how the job will benefit you. This way, you're showing you are a team player, and separating yourself from the many other applications who will be me-me-me focused.

Try sentences like: "With my background in A, B and C, I will be an asset to your company's success in X, Y and Z." Or, perhaps, "As your organization builds its reputation as a leader in X, my strengths in A, B and C will enable me to be a valuable contributor from the start."

the quote, but do you know what comes after that? "And it must follow, as the night the day, thou canst not then be false to any man." Translation: If you are honest with yourself, you'll be honest with others.

Benjamin Franklin believed the same thing. "We can never choose evil, as evil, but under the appearance of an imaginary good," he said. Franklin believed that the core of dishonesty was that you have to be dishonest with yourself before you are ever dishonest with others—convincing yourself some bad deed is acceptable, making excuses for your shortcomings, lying to yourself to make it easier to lie to others.

Find Balance at Work

Part of doing honest work and succeeding is finding your personal balance. The WTFers who tested out work-focused advice added a

Out-of-Date Language, Totally Current Advice from Samuel Smiles's Duty

"Noble work is the true educator. Idleness is a thorough demoralizer of body, soul and conscience. Nine-tenths of the vices and miseries of the world proceed from idleness. Without work, there can be no active progress in human welfare."

"Every generation has to bear its own burden, to weather its peculiar perils, to pass through its manifold trials. We are daily exposed to temptations, whether it be of idleness, self-indulgence or vice. . . . When virtue has thus become a daily habit, we become possessed of an individual character, prepared for fulfilling, in great measure, the ends for which we were created."

"How many tricks are resorted to—in which honesty forms no part—for making money faster than others. Instead of working patiently and well for a modest living, many desire to get rich all at once. The spirit of the age is not that of a trader, but of a gambler. The pace is too fast to allow of any one stopping to inquire as to those who have fallen out of the way. . . . Young business men are often carried away by such examples. If they have no firmness and courage . . . they become dishonest and unscrupulous."

tidbit from M. Scott Peck, *The Road Less Traveled*, to the mix: Balance means patience with yourself and with the world around you, writes Peck. It means controlling your anger, and recognizing the role of faith in your life. Balance requires discipline and feeds a disciplined life.

If you're getting frustrated at work, step back and ask yourself why. Is it necessary to express your frustration right there and then, or can you channel that emotion to get the changes you want in a more constructive way? Finding balance and being even-keeled in your emotional reactions, WTFers reported, was a good skill to remember.

Kim found the balance section of Peck's advice most useful because it helped her deal with anger at work, where she manages several others. With a short temper, "it has been difficult for me to keep my cool at work because I find it very easy to get angry when people make mistakes or are lazy," she said.

After reading the Peck advice, and attempting better balance of emotions, she drastically reduced the amount of stress she felt at work. "Instead of jumping the gun and getting angry, I've tried to ask myself whether or not it is necessary for me to express anger in certain situations. With further reflection and finding that it is not necessary, I've found that my anger subsides and I approach the situation more calmly. Because I am challenged daily with the urge to become angry, it has required serious commitment and perseverance to be able to step outside the situation and approach it from a different angle." Becoming a Wise, Tenacious, and Fearless you is something you do for yourself, sure, but it's also something you do to strengthen the relationships you have with others. Armed with these tips for getting a good job and acing interviews, it's also important to think about your personal relationships—with friends, loved ones, and neighbors—and how being fearless in your values and purpose can have a positive impact on others along the way.

Honest Interest at Work Yields Rewards

Lizzie used Carnegie's advice about showing sincere interest to boost her business as a cosmetics consultant at the local mall. "My new goals, using Carnegie's advice, were to spend more time with my customers which will allow me to get to know them better, put more emphasis on the people and less on the products, and finally, just be more interested in people. The one thing I want my customers to understand is that I actually care more about them getting the results they want and less on making a sale."

Over the course of a month, Lizzie tried Carnegie's advice to become genuinely interested in others, and said she developed new relationships with customers. "I have only had positive results with this piece of advice; there was never an instance where it failed. For example, while I am doing a consultation I have lots of time to get to know someone. I am amazed at just how much the customers will share with us. A woman had made an appointment with me just to come in and play around and while I was doing the consultation I just made small talk: What do you do? Do you go to school? I ended up finding out we had a lot in common: We are both dating guys that are older, and we discussed about how people react to it and just about the odd things that go along with it." Lizzie said that customer has returned three or four times since.

Carnegie's advice has also boosted her commissions. "When I took the time to get to know my customers and become genuinely interested in them I did have bigger sales. People are more likely to spend money (which has become very precious in this economy) when they feel like I am more interested in their concerns and them as a person and not just the sale. Not only have I enjoyed the financial benefits of this advice, but I have had a great time getting to know people. I would say that I have actually made friends just not customers which is a good feeling. People are coming to us for the service not just the products."

Chapter 8 encourages you to be fearless by getting outside yourself, by forming strong relationships, and using your gifts to help others.

This chapter offered a lot of tips and advice. Reading it is only the first step. To become fearless in your job interviews, workplace experiences, and personal life will mean putting some or all of these techniques into action. So make a commitment here and now:

In my next job interview (or my next interaction with a professor or work colleague) I will try the following bits of advice

I'm going to follow this advice   **on page ...**

_____   p. # _____

_____   p. # _____

_____   p. # _____

In my next interaction with friends, family or my significant other, I will try the following bits of advice

I'm going to follow this advice   **on page ...**

_____   p. # _____

_____   p. # _____

_____   p. # _____

Make Meaning

Thinking Outside the "You" Box

It's survey time once more:

For each, choose A or B.

1. A. I have a natural talent for influencing people.
    B. I am not good at influencing people.

2. A. Modesty doesn't become me.
    B. I am essentially a modest person.

3. A. I would do almost anything on a dare.
    B. I tend to be a fairly cautious person.

4. A. When people compliment me I sometimes get embarrassed.
    B. I know that I am good because everybody keeps telling me so.

5. A. The thought of ruling the world frightens the hell out of me.
    B. If I ruled the world it would be a better place.

6. A. I can usually talk my way out of anything.
    B. I try to accept the consequences of my behavior.

7. A. I prefer to blend in with the crowd.
    B. I like to be the center of attention.

8. A. I will be a success.
    B. I am not too concerned about success.

9. A. I am no better or worse than most people.
   B. I think I am a special person.

10. A. I am not sure if I would make a good leader.
    B. I see myself as a good leader.

11. A. I am assertive.
    B. I wish I were more assertive.

12. A. I like to have authority over other people.
    B. I don't mind following orders.

13. A. I find it easy to manipulate people.
    B. I don't like it when I find myself manipulating people.

14. A. I insist upon getting the respect that is due to me.
    B. I usually get the respect that I deserve.

15. A. I don't particularly like to show off my body.
    B. I like to show off my body.

16. A. I can read people like a book.
    B. People are sometimes hard to understand.

17. A. If I feel competent I am willing to take responsibility for making decisions.
    B. I like to take responsibility for making decisions.

18. A. I just want to be reasonably happy.
    B. I want to amount to something in the eyes of the world.

19. A. My body is nothing special.
    B. I like to look at my body.

20. A. I try not to be a show-off.
    B. I will usually show off if I get the chance.

21. A. I always know what I am doing.
    B. Sometimes I am not sure of what I am doing.

22. A. I sometimes depend on people to get things done.
    B. I rarely depend on anyone else to get things done.

23. A. Sometimes I tell good stories.
    B. Everybody likes to hear my stories.

24. A. I expect a great deal from other people.
    B. I like to do things for other people.

25. A. I will never be satisfied until I get all that I deserve.
    B. I take my satisfactions as they come.

26. A. Compliments embarrass me.
    B. I like to be complimented.

27. A. I have a strong will to power.
    B. Power for its own sake doesn't interest me.

28. A. I don't care about new fads and fashions.
    B. I like to start new fads and fashions.

29. A. I like to look at myself in the mirror.
    B. I am not particularly interested in looking at myself in the mirror.

30. A. I really like to be the center of attention.
    B. It makes me uncomfortable to be the center of attention.

31. A. I can live my life in any way I want to.
    B. People can't always live their lives in terms of what they want.

32. A. Being an authority doesn't mean that much to me.
    B. People always seem to recognize my authority.

33. A. I would prefer to be a leader.
    B. It makes little difference to me whether I am a leader or not.

34. A. I am going to be a great person.
    B. I hope I am going to be successful.

35. A. People sometimes believe what I tell them.
    B. I can make anybody believe anything I want them to.

36. A. I am a born leader.
    B. Leadership is a quality that takes a long time to develop.

37. A. I wish somebody would someday write my biography.
    B. I don't like people to pry into my life for any reason.

38. A. I get upset when people don't notice how I look when I go out in public.
    B. I don't mind blending into the crowd when I go out in public.

39. A. I am more capable than other people.
    B. There is a lot that I can learn from other people.

40. A. I am much like everybody else.
    B. I am an extraordinary person.

SCORING KEY:

Assign one point for each response that matches the key.

1, 2, and 3:	A	16:	A		29, 30, 31:	A	
4, 5:	B	17, 18, 19, 20:	B		32:	B	
6:	A	21:	A		33, 34:	A	
7:	B	22, 23:	B		35:	B	
8:	A	24, 25:	A		36, 37, 38, 39:	A	
9, 10:	B	26:	B		40:	B	
11, 12, 13, 14:	A	27:	A				
15:	B	28:	B				

TOTAL SCORE

Want to learn more about your score and what it tells you about your authority, self-sufficiency, superiority, and vanity? Go to www .generationwtf.com to find out more details.

Congratulations. You just took a narcissism inventory. And odds are, you're pretty self-absorbed. Are you more navel-gazing than your parents—or even folks just a decade or two older than you? Based on the results of the narcissistic personality inventory, a standardized test that has been given to students at the University of South Alabama over the last fifteen years, the answer is yes.

Narcissists are people who think very highly of themselves, are self-absorbed, and have unrealistic views about their own qualities and little regard for others. Sounds like a lot of people you know, right? What was your score on the test above? The higher the score, the more narcissistic you are. (For your generation, the mean results seem to fall in the 15–17 range.)

Looking inward for honest self-appraisal is good stuff. But unless you give of yourself and have rich interactions with others, things will get ugly pretty fast. Good relationships with your friends, family, and community mean getting out of your "I'm fabulous" mode and thinking about others first. You know this . . . but a reminder of exactly how to do it was very helpful for Generation WTFers I surveyed.

This chapter will help you

▶ Create more **meaningful friendships** by amping up your listening skills;
▶ Create more **meaningful relationships** (with significant others and loved ones) by learning the research behind five common questions; and
▶ Create more **meaningful communities** by getting involved in volunteer and charity work.

Create More Meaningful Friendships

Friendships are important. According to Generation WTF surveys, you rank being loyal to your friends as the number one value in your life.

Indeed, it's our friends who get us through some of the toughest times of our twenties—and it can also be drama with said friends that causes the most heartache. WTF testers tried advice from *How to Win Friends and Influence People*, *The 7 Habits of Highly Effective People*, and *59 Seconds: Think a Little, Change a Lot*, settling on these top three tips to create thriving friendships.

Be Present

I want to know how to connect with people on a more personal level. I think today this is something that is becoming more of an issue. With texting and Facebook and the Internet and all of that, I feel as though there is a personalness that is being lost when people try to connect. So how can we be less awkward? —Martin

Try this: Prioritize in-person conversations and don't multitask when you're talking with someone. How many times have you played video games while talking on the phone with your parents? Guess what, they can tell you're not all there. Feel just a bit slighted when a friend sends a long text message while the two of you are talking about something important? Don't do it.

This isn't earth-shattering advice, but WTF testers were surprised by what a big impact being present had in their personal lives. Writes Dale Carnegie, "If you want others to like you, if you want to develop real friendships, if you want to help others at the same time as you help yourself, keep this principle in mind: Become genuinely interested in other people."

Taking time to show honest interest in others means asking questions and listening to the answers. It means carving out old-fashioned face time with someone—and not doing anything else other than being with that person.

Generation WTF Gets Present

Turn off your "stuff"—your cell phone, iPad, iPhone, BlackBerry, etc. And I don't mean just putting 'em on vibrate. There is an on/off switch for this very reason. "It's really hard to do the first couple of times, but my best friend and I were drifting apart and this made a difference. We don't have a lot of time together, so we wanted to make it count," said Kristin.

Go for a walk. It's easier for some people to put aside distractions when they take a walk in a park or on quiet neighborhood streets. You're multitasking in some ways—burning calories while having quality time—but it also allows both of you to get away from other people for a bit.

Listen. Sara said being reminded to simply listen to her friend talk—without interrupting or deflecting the conversation onto her own interests—made her friend "overjoyed." This worked so well that she tried it with a guy she met one night at a bar. As he talked about his work, she made sure to listen and ask questions. "He, too, was completely excited about the conversation and had a smile the entire time he was speaking," Sara concluded. "[Carnegie's] advice does pay off when talking to others; it keeps them more interested and involved in a conversation. The actions that Carnegie taught me also made me feel better about myself because I was able to share a different experience with loved ones and make a new acquaintance that I would otherwise probably not have. The ideas that I implemented not only let others share their lives with me and made them happy, but it also gave me a refreshing feeling to make someone smile. The advice works in many positive ways. Carnegie makes valid points to many situations, whether in an average conversation with someone you are already close to or in an instance when you are trying to make a new friend."

It's Okay to Be Trusting

In lab settings and in opinion polls, we tend to report thinking that other people are less trustworthy than we are. But a 2010 study by psychologists Detlef Fetchenhauer and David Dunning suggests that we just don't have enough practice trusting people because we're stuck in a vicious cycle of cynicism.

When people are shown the trust of others, their trust increases, the researchers found. So show some trust to others, and they are more likely to behave in a kind and trusting way toward you.

Limit Your "Gossip Girl Persona"

We all know gossip is bad. But I bet you didn't know that when you say negative things about someone else, the person you're talking to is more likely to think negatively about you, too. It's a weird quirk of our psychology called "spontaneous trait transference": When you gossip about how bad or weird or ugly someone else is, the person you're talking to will start thinking those things about you. In his book 59 *Seconds*, psychologist Richard Wiseman cites this research and advises readers to stop complaining so much about other people—by being nicer to others, you're actually making yourself look better, too. Some seventy-five years earlier, without the benefit of psychological proof, Dale Carnegie seemed to understand this, too: Rather than "criticize, condemn or complain," it's best to "try to understand [people]. Let's try to figure out why they do what they do," Carnegie advised.

Regardless of the packaging, WTFers who tried to do this for a few weeks noticed nearly instant rewards. Said Lauren, a WTF tester who really embraced this tip: "Gossip is a staple piece of my conversations with friends. I think a lot of people pepper their normal communication with gossip to seem relatable and to add an air of humor to the discussion. When I made an effort to limit my 'gossip girl persona,' my friends began to gossip less, too. My friends kept saying I was 'so nice.' It showed that my lack of petty chit chat did have an impact on the way people viewed me, even among my closest friends. And I increased my likeability factor." But it was no cake walk.

Sarah said she initially thought Carnegie's book was "simplistic, commonsense advice," and thought following Carnegie's advice against

XOXO: Tips to Stop the Gossip

- ▶ **Carry a reminder:** Sara wore a bracelet on her right wrist and she'd transfer it to the left when she gossiped.

- ▶ **Write it down:** Keep track of when you are being negative and reward yourself for a full day of gossip-free talk.

- ▶ **Turn it into a contest:** Pair up with a friend and monitor each other. The first one to gossip or say something negative about someone else has to buy the other person ice cream.

criticizing, condemning, and complaining would be simple. "I had no idea how much I complained," she said, after trying out the advice for a few days. Even when she was trying to remain positive, her roommates complained constantly about how much work they had to do, and soon she said she'd "jump in and add my issues to the list." She hasn't given up yet, though.

"Seek First to Understand, Then to Be Understood"

How do I deal with the living habits of crazy roommates? They are keeping tabs on me and getting into my business. —Kayla

Living with others can be challenging. And living with others who aren't necessarily your best friends makes it even more awkward. But take a moment to think about why your roommates are acting crazy. Are they trying to become friends with you? What are they hoping to accomplish? Trying to really *understand* your roommates will be a great start to reducing the crazy factor around the house.

Most of us listen to others just enough so that we can think of a reply. Then we spend most of our time thinking about how we're going to advise or criticize or react to what the other person is saying, rather than actually listening and seeking to understand the full meaning. In *The 7 Habits of Highly Effective People*, Stephen Covey advises readers to practice "empathic listening"—listening to understand—and stresses that the ability to listen is very much within our control. (Getting others to do the same so they understand you, well, that's somewhat more challenging.)

Dale Carnegie offered similar advice when he told readers to express sincere interest in others. These bits of advice, taken together, "had a big impact"—especially for those dealing with difficult roommates.

Rachel was living with a woman whom she didn't get along with very well. Her roommate seemed to be sort of an outcast and had a boyfriend Rachel didn't really like. However, Rachel said that she has no personal animosity toward this roommate—it was just one of those awkward relationships for no good reason. So she decided to reach out.

"Usually, I would not go out of my way to say hello or ask how she is doing, but I decided to commit to being honestly interested in her. It amazed me to see how positively she responded to my interest; once a quiet girl, she was now a girl that I could not get to stop talking. She had an endless amount of stories and issues that she was waiting for someone to ask her about so that she could vent, even if it was as simple as something that happened at work that day. I found that in return she did several nice things for me that none of my other roommates would ever consider doing for me, such as driving me thirty miles away just to drop me off and turn around to head straight to work, or help me with an art project. They were actions I did not expect as a result of appreciating her presence and making her feel important by acknowledging her and listening to her. A good friendship has bloomed just by simply deciding to honestly care about and take an interest in someone. Overall, this advice really paid off and it will continue to pay off because it is an easy thing to do once you are aware of the positive benefits of such simple acts."

Jaye said she turned a tumultuous relationship with her roommate back into a friendship this way, too. "To me it seemed that my roommate and I were both steaming under the surface. I am a messy person, whereas my roommate is a very neat and meticulous person, I am a night owl and she is an early bird, and that is just the start of how different we are. These differences can really start to wear a person down and I felt like my roommate was being more negatively affected by it than I was. So after one evening of my roommate crying herself to sleep for an unknown reason, I decided it was time we reconnected since it had been quite some time since the last heart-to-heart we had had. While the conversation initially started as a tell-all for her, it turned into discussing this last year and how we felt about it. She admitted that while in the beginning it was hard for her to deal with living with someone who is as messy as I can be, I have other positive qualities and that really made me realize that we are just different. No one is better in the way they do stuff or the things they choose; we are simply different, and we both have learned to appreciate each other."

Carnegie and Covey's advice "definitely opened my eyes to new ways for me to interpret things and new ways to make me more personable and—dare I say it—*charming*," Jaye said.

How's Your Empathy?

How much do you agree with these statements?

- ▶ "I sometimes try to understand my friends better by imagining how things look from their perspective."
- ▶ "I often have tender, concerned feelings for people less fortunate than me."

Does that sound like you? Or not so much? According to a recent University of Michigan study college students today don't have as much empathy—the ability to understand and enter into another person's feelings—as college students of the 1980s and 1990s. "College kids today are about 40 percent lower in empathy than their counterparts of 20 or 30 years ago, as measured by standard tests of this personality trait," reported Sara Konrath, a researcher at the University of Michigan Institute for Social Research.

Compared with studies of young adults in the late 1970s, your generation is much less likely to agree with those two empathy statements

Empathic Listening 101

Here are some great places to try out your empathic listening skills:

When a friend comes to you with a personal problem. Try listening first, rather than just telling him what to do immediately. Chris did this with a lot of success: Usually, he would have jumped in and started firing off advice. "Instead I really tried to understand the problem from his perspective. While I didn't have an answer for him, he said that he felt much better knowing someone could understand what he was going through. I thought this was really amazing, because even though I couldn't possibly relate to what he was going through, by listening empathically I was able to provide a channel of communication that allowed him to work through his own issue."

When you're at a noisy bar. Stephen Covey suggests honing your listening skills by watching people to get a sense for what their body language can tell you. Katherine tried this and "even without hearing the words of the conversation between people I could still figure out the basics of what the people were saying. Actions such as holding hands or hugging speak louder than words to express a feeling. People have different actions towards different people depending on their relationship with each other."

Behavior Is Contagious: Pick Your Friends Wisely

We generally understand how a virus or flu spreads: I'm sick and I shake hands with you. Then, you touch your nose and . . . oops, now you're sick, too. Then you kiss your boyfriend and . . . oops, now he's sick, too. And so on. But in recent years, social scientists have begun to consider whether behaviors and character traits can spread in a similar way. Turns out that many behaviors are similarly "contagious."

Researchers Nicholas Christakis, a medical sociologist, and James Fowler, a political science professor, have found that obesity is contagious: We're more likely to gain weight ourselves if our family and friends gain weight. Similarly, we're more likely to succeed in losing weight if others are trying to do the same. Loneliness and happiness are similarly spreadable. The list goes on: You're more likely to drink a lot if your friends do, too. And on a positive note, kindness is catchy, too, giving new power to the idea of "paying it forward" in generosity.

All this research gives new meaning to the Golden Rule about doing unto others as you would have them do unto you. And to your parents' admonitions about finding some "nice" friends to play with. It's so annoying when God and your parents were right all along. So go find some nice friends. Just don't be drinking when you do!

above. (Want to test yourself, get your empathy score, and find out how you compare with others? You'll find links to online surveys at www.generationwtf.com.)

Having empathy for others is a big part of getting fearless: It's about embracing the meaningful relationships that Generation WTF seeks. Rachel, Chris, and Jaye exhibited empathy in how they handled their roommates and friends during tough times. And when Stephen Covey talks about empathic listening, he's talking about engaging with people in a way they feel heard, focusing on subtle cues and body language. The goal in acting with empathy is to make the other person feel safe and valued. Sometimes that means listening to a friend vent for a while before offering advice. Other times it means asking open-ended questions, nodding as the person talks, and thinking about things from their perspective.

Try some of the tricks outlined in this chapter to boost your empathy, and check out the resources section at the end of the book for more guides to empathic living.

Create More Meaningful Relationships

For the last four years, I've taught a class on the sociology of marriage and family. After we cover the history and research, Generation WTFers always have a lot of questions: What do people look for in relationships? When is the right time for sex? After college, where do you meet someone? How do I know who the right match is for me? If I'm living with my boyfriend, is that okay? Why won't my partner help with the housework? And the list goes on.

There are thousands of self-help books out there about relationships, but here are the top five bits of new research that can help you in your quest for lasting love:

1. What do men and women want in a long-term relationship?

Here's the short answer: Among Generation WTFers, men are increasingly interested in an educated woman who is a good financial prospect. Women are increasingly interested in a man who wants a family and less picky about whether he's always Mr. Nice Guy.

That's according to a study that I conducted with Christie Boxer, a

Sometimes the Best Advice Is to Keep Your Mouth Shut

WTF tester Julie said after testing out the "tough love" advice that Phil McGraw recommends in *Life Strategies*, she realized "people do not always want to hear the honest truth. Many times people ask for opinions just because they want to get reassurance and gain acceptance." When her sister called crying about a guy who she'd been having problems with for several months, Julie said, "[I] figured she needed to 'get real' and hear the brutal and honest truth. I lectured her about how she was wasting her time because this guy clearly did not like her; otherwise he would be treating her like a princess and they would be officially boyfriend and girlfriend. I told her to wake up and get a sense of reality, this guy was a loser and she could do better. At first the results were effective, she agreed with me and thanked me for the reality check and she began to take action. However, two days later when I talked to her she timidly admitted that she was now dating the guy she was complaining about. I was going to start reprimanding her, but I realized that no matter what I would say to her she was not going to listen to me because she did not care what I had to say about it. All she wanted was to let me know that this was the situation now and she wanted my acceptance and approval. No amount of 'get real' speeches would change her mind. That is when I officially decided to give up Dr. Phil's 'get real' idea of honesty and stick with Dale Carnegie's advice."

graduate student at the University of Iowa. We analyzed results from a 2008 survey of more than 1,100 undergraduates at the University of Iowa, the University of Washington, the University of Virginia, and Penn State University, comparing the results to past mate-preference studies.

Since the 1930s, researchers have been asking college students to rank a list of eighteen characteristics they'd prefer in a mate from "irrelevant" (0) to "essential" (3), allowing for a comparison of mate preferences dating back three generations. And my, how times have changed: Generation WTF ranks love and attraction as most important; a few generations ago it didn't even make the top three.

What Men Want

Marriage used to be a practical arrangement: Getting married for love or attraction was considered foolish and perhaps even dangerous. So in the 1930s male respondents were seeking a dependable, kind lady who had skills in the kitchen. They ranked chastity as more important than intelligence.

Fast-forward seven decades: Now guys look for love, brains, and beauty—and a sizable salary certainly sweetens the deal. Generation WTF men ranked "good financial prospect" number twelve in 2008, a significant climb from seventeen in 1939 and eighteen in 1967. In times of economic difficulty, it's no wonder that guys want someone with whom to share the burden of financial responsibility.

Chastity—which men ranked at ten in 1939—fell to dead last in 2008 for both men and women. In fact, when we administered the survey, several female students snickered at the idea that we even included the chastity item. This is consistent with the widespread hook-up culture on college campuses—and it's not a great trend. Chastity before marriage increases the likelihood of a lasting, happy relationship and decreases the likelihood of divorce, according to research by W. Bradford Wilcox, a professor at the University of Virginia. "Successful marriages are built in part around the virtue of sexual fidelity and against a horizon of commitment—both of which are most easily realized in the bonds of wedlock."

For Generation WTF, part of being Wise and Fearless is making smart choices about the future. This trend might be worth reconsidering in your own personal life.

What Women Want

There's a great stand-up routine from Chris Rock where he says that he's figured out what women want:

Everything.

That's not quite true (but it's still funny).

For women of the 1930s, emotional stability, dependable character, and ambition ranked as the top three characteristics they wanted in a man. Attraction and love didn't come in until number five. Today, women, like men, put love at the top of the list, with dependability and emotional stability rounding out the top three characteristics in Mr. Right.

Women rate desire for home and children much higher in importance than men do. In 2008 women rated desire for home and children fourth; men ranked it ninth. And women ranked "pleasing disposition" as significantly less important in 2008 than ever before. Pleasing disposition—presumably interpreted to mean being a nice guy—fell from a steady ranking of four throughout the second half of the twentieth century to a significantly lower rank of seven in 2008.

Perhaps this means WTF women are more forgiving if their boyfriend or husband forgets chocolates and flowers on Valentine's Day, as long as he meets the other requirements she's looking for in a guy. Maybe? Possibly? (The guys out there are shaking their heads, especially if they're still in the doghouse for getting their spouse or girlfriend something that plugged in instead of something sparkly.)

But more likely, this points to a change in vocabulary: "Pleasing disposition" is a very old-fashioned phrase that might not be the most accurate measure of modern preferences.

On the next page, check out the table of what men and women want—throughout the last seven decade Then go online at www.gen erationwtf.com to create your own ranking and compare it with the rankings of others.

2. After college, where do I meet someone?

According to a Pew Internet and American Life Project survey, only 13 percent of couples who are married or in a serious long-term relationship met at a bar, nightclub, café, or other social gathering. The most common places to meet a match were work or school groups and introductions through family and friends. After that, online dating and speed dating becomes pretty common, too. But it's never easy.

Do you daydream about to walking into a big room with one hundred eligible partners there for you to choose from? That would make it so much easier, right? That implausible scenario led to some fascinating research about whether the fishing is better in big or small ponds.

So here's a scenario for you:

You are a single person looking for a mate with a good education and positive values. You would also like to be with someone physically attractive. You're out of college and in a new city, so you sign up for a

RANK ORDERING OF MATE PREFERENCES ACROSS SEVEN DECADES, BY PARTICIPANT GENDER

Characteristic	Men							Women						
	1939	1956	1967	1977	1984/1985	1996	2008	1939	1956	1967	1977	1984/1985	1996	2008
Dependable character	1	1	1	3	3	2	2	2	1	2	3	3	2	2
Emotional stability, maturity	2	2	3	1	2	3	3	1	2	1	2	2	3	3
Pleasing disposition	3	4	4	4	4	4	5	4	5	4	4	4	4	7
Mutual attraction, love	4	3	2	2	1	1	1	5	6	3	1	1	1	1
Good health	5	6	9	5	6	6	7	6	9	10	8	9	9	9
Desire for home, children	6	5	5	11	9	9	9	7	3	5	10	7	6	4
Refinement, neatness	7	8	7	10	10	11	11	8	7	8	12	12	12	13
Good cook, housekeeper	8	7	6	13	13	14	13	16	16	16	16	16	16	15
Ambition, industriousness	9	9	8	8	11	10	10	3	4	6	6	6	7	8
Chastity	10	13	15	17	17	16	18	10	15	15	18	18	17	18
Education, intelligence	11	11	10	7	5	5	4	9	14	7	5	5	5	5
Sociability	12	12	12	6	8	7	6	11	11	13	7	8	8	6
Similar religious background	13	14	13	14	12	12	16	14	10	11	13	15	14	14
Good looks	14	15	11	9	7	8	8	17	18	17	15	13	13	12
Similar education background	15	14	13	12	12	12	14	12	8	9	9	10	10	11
Favorable social status	16	16	16	15	14	17	15	15	13	14	14	14	15	16
Good financial prospect	17	17	18	16	16	13	12	13	12	12	11	11	11	10
Similar political background	18	18	17	18	18	18	17	18	17	18	17	17	18	17

Honesty Is the Best Policy: Relationships Edition

Christopher had proposed to his fiancée a few months earlier, and the wedding plans were underway. But then his ex-girlfriend appeared out of nowhere, and the two began corresponding, then meeting secretly. While things never progressed past clandestine talks, Christopher knew that his behavior was dishonest. And then his fiancée found out. He said he'd stop spending time with his ex, but then continued to meet with the other woman for several weeks.

"I lied to my fiancée multiple times, to the point where she could no longer trust me," he said, and she gave back her engagement ring. Christopher had been "bored" by Dale Carnegie's *How to Win Friends and Influence People*. But with his love life in tatters, he decided he needed some advice.

He turned to Carnegie's passages on admitting mistakes before criticizing others. "I have made a lot of mistakes in my life, and just recently I have only started to share them," he said, after pondering the book's advice. He spoke to his fiancée and came clean with the truth, begging forgiveness. And it worked.

"After almost losing the woman I loved, I learned that you can't always have your cake and eat it too. If you are hurting someone you care for because you are doing something you know you shouldn't—like talking to an ex-girlfriend who wants you all to herself—then stop. It is not worth hurting the ones you love simply because you like the attention. The lesson I learned from the past week will stick with me for the rest of my life, and I will share that lesson to anyone who wishes to hear it, or to those who are in the situation I just got out of," Christopher said.

All of his lies had "come back to bite" him and toward the end of the semester, he presented his findings on honesty other WTF testers. "Dale Carnegie got me out of some real trouble," he told his classmates. "And I'm totally converted to the virtue of honesty."

speed-dating service, where you have brief conversations with potential partners. You (and potential partners with similar criteria) are *less* likely to focus on physical attributes and pay more attention to intelligence and values if:

a. There are twelve potential dates at the event;

b. there are twenty-four potential dates at the event;

c. there are thirty-six potential dates at the event;

d. there are more than thirty-six potential dates at the event.

The correct answer is *A*. Fishing in a smaller pond makes you more likely to focus on what's really important, while having lots of choices encourages you to focus on superficial elements of a person's presentation, like height and weight.

This little puzzle was put together by journalist Shankar Vedantam, author of *The Hidden Brain*, based on research from Alison Lenton at the University of Edinburgh and Marco Francesconi at the University of Essex, who studied eighty-four speed-dating events.

Bottom line: Our brains can't pay attention to everything at once. So while you'd think it would be better to have tons of choices of people to date, actually, fishing in a smaller pond helps you make better decisions.

3. How do I know who the right "match" is for me?

This is the one question I can't answer with research, except to say when you've found it, you'll know. However, one of the most common mistakes we make in our early days of dating is that we lose ourselves in the process of trying to please others. Remember, you're not looking to "win" some game. You're looking to make a strong, lifelong match.

Q *I may be a little shy at times, but I do not consider myself socially inept. I can chat up just about any girl that I have interest in, but I've never been in a relationship. I don't have a problem with asking girls out that I only have a limited interest in. It's simply that, when the stakes are high, I fold. If I really like them, I simply end up letting them go. What can I do to fix this? —Tom*

A Part of the fear of rejection is a fear of the unknown. We worry about how terrible we'll feel and create nightmare scenarios in our head. But, while it certainly hurts to be shot down, in reality, it's not going to end your social life. In avoiding relationships, you can shield yourself from the possibility of rejection by never opening up, never admitting your feelings, and while that might prevent rejection, it also prevents meaningful and fulfilling human interactions. And *now* we're talking about things to fear: If you never try, you certainly won't succeed. If you never open your heart to give love to a special person, you're not going to get those warm and fuzzy feelings back atcha.

To fear regret more than rejection means to stop playing the "No, I don't think of you that way" scenarios in your head. Instead, try this mental exercise: Fast forward to meeting this person twenty years from now, admitting your crush from college and having them say, "Oh, I felt the same way. I wish you'd said something . . ."

Now *that's* crushing.

Before you can say "I love you," you must first learn how to say the "I." This is the only honest way one can wish to be loved.

Think of it like you're casting a movie—you need the lead character in this romantic drama. Well, that's you. You are the star of your own life. You make things happen: Your personality, your dreams, your choices. So that means you need to learn what success means for you, how to carry yourself with confidence.

Once you know who you are and what you want, it's time to find your life costar. Going back through your values is a good way to begin: You're looking for someone who shares your life outlook, who will share your dreams, and who will be a strong companion through good times and bad.

4. Living together is a good idea to see if you are compatible, right?

Wrong. There's no research that shows that living together increases your odds of a happy, healthy marriage. At best, if you cohabit with only one person—and then get married to that person—it's less likely to have a negative effect. But it ain't helping.

The vast majority of Generation WTFers want to get married some-day. As you navigate your twenties, building careers and searching for soul mates, you might delay that goal yet still want to experience inti-mate relationships. So that's where living together seems appealing. Many people think of these long-term relationships as an "internship" for marriage: You want to test it out, have some of the fun without all the commitment, and see if it's right for you. Here's the problem: Research clearly shows that living with more than one partner doubles your odds of divorce in the future.

Communication is key. Do you see a future with this person? Talk about it. Don't make assumptions just to avoid an awkward conversa-tion: Men and women often think about living together in different ways. Here's some news you can use: Women tend to think of liv-ing together as a step toward marriage—an increase in the commit-

Communication Is Key

According to studies, men and women have different ideas of the "significance" of moving in together. Just because you think living together is a step toward marriage and an increase in the depth of your relationship doesn't mean your partner is on the same page.

ment of the relationship. Men, however, don't always share that view: According to research by University of Michigan sociologist Pamela Smock, men may see the new arrangements as a lateral move to test out whether a "next step" seems like a good idea.

5. I need advice on relationships generally. Why does it seem like nothing is ever easy?

In *How to Win Friends and Influence People*, Dale Carnegie tells dozens of stories in an attempt to convince readers of the old adage that you can catch more flies with honey than vinegar: Being nice to people, thanking them for their efforts, and showing honest appreciation can work wonders in your business *and* personal relationships. Showing appreciation can yield big results.

Appreciate your family. Ask *them* questions—and show interest in their lives. In many families, it's the children who are the center of attention. When was the last time you asked your parents how they are doing, what's going on with their jobs, or even just how their day was? "Through the years my father has always done the question asking, while I do the responding," said Sara. Even when her father would talk, she usually brought the conversation back to a topic of interest to her. But applying Carnegie's advice, she took a different tack. "He recently has been very involved with purchasing a condo out of state. He brought up the subject recently and I made sure to ask as many questions as immediately came to my mind. Instead of letting the subject change or offering my input, I continued to ask him things about why he wanted to do this and what he was looking for. Even though he is one of the closest people to me, his interest in the conversation grew. He was increasingly involved in talking to me and his mood was ecstatic as I continued to ask questions."

Jodi said she followed that same advice at Easter dinner with her grandmother. "I listened intently and with great enthusiasm. I spoke of her thoughts and then my opinions. We ended up having a very good conversation that I would have otherwise missed out on due to my inability to be a good listener."

Appreciate your significant other. Yes, he or she may drive you crazy sometimes. But Dale Carnegie's advice was helpful for WTF relationships. Erin said she interpreted Carnegie's advice as simply an extension of the Golden Rule: Treat others as you'd like to be treated. She used Carnegie's advice most often with her fiancé, with whom she lives. While she'd like to see the cleaning, cooking, and laundry done before relaxing for the evening, she said her fiancé "more often than not, sits on the couch and watches television until he goes to bed. However, every now and again, when he has a day off of work or is home by himself for a while, I will come home to a spotless apartment."

Erin said she hadn't rewarded those spotless-apartment moments enough because she felt he shouldn't have to be thanked for doing his fair share. But after reading Carnegie, Erin wondered if her "lack of sincere appreciation may be part of the reason he does not help out that much, so I decided to test out Carnegie's advice by showing sincere appreciation. I had had a really busy and stressful week at school and we had visitors coming to stay with us that weekend and the apartment was a mess. When I returned home from my Friday classes, my

Top Tip to Get Your Girlfriend's Parents to Like You: Show Genuine Interest

Nick, who was raised in the suburbs of Chicago, said he knew nothing about farming, so when he spent the day with his girlfriend's stepfather—a farmer—he started asking questions. "My goal was to get him to warm up to me. I attempted to do this by talking about his passion." Nick recalled a vignette from *How to Win Friends and Influence People* about a man who won the friendship of judge by appealing to the judge's love of dog breeding. While the man had no background in show dogs, he was able to listen and learn from the judge, winning his friendship.

Similarly, Nick said that after a "few basic questions," the farmer stepfather talked for ninety minutes about his work. "He ended up warming up to me simply because I let him talk about what interested him. This is what Carnegie was getting at . . . talk to people in a sincere manner and you will raise their impression of you."

fiancé had cleaned the whole place for me so that I could come home and relax. Instead of telling him that he should do that more often, I smiled big, thanked him many times, and complimented him profusely on how good of a job he had done. Now he is much more inclined to

Get Fearless, Carnegie Style

"When I was reading Dale Carnegie's *How to Win Friends and Influence People* back in February I remember how excited and motivated I was to put a quality effort into becoming more aware of my relations and gestures with others," said Gina. "I was surprised by the amount of impact the book had made on the way I thought about communicating with others and my own personal feelings." Gina said she learned to "have a greater appreciation for the modest triumphs in life and not take the little things for granted anymore. As graduation approaches I have found myself taking advantage of being more honest with myself and preparing for a new lifestyle as I move on with my life. Dale Carnegie's timeless advice has helped me take a step back, relax, and evaluate the important aspects of the relationships and interactions I share with others."

help me out because he was able to see how happy it made me and it made him feel good to do something nice and be recognized for how well he did it."

Create More Meaningful Communities

More than 90 percent of the Generation WTFers I surveyed said they'd be much more satisfied with their lives if they felt like they were doing more to make a difference in their community. (In comparison, only 14 percent said they'd be much more satisfied with their lives if they had a nicer car.)

Odds are you were raised with the idea that giving back—volunteering, being good to your community and your environment—was important. Perhaps the more cynical among you saw this as just another line on your resume to get into a good college, but surveys show people born between 1982 and 2000 are the most civic-minded since the generation of the 1930s and 1940s, Morley Winograd and Michael Hais, coauthors of *Millennial Makeover: MySpace, YouTube, and the Future of American Politics*, told *USA Today*.

Even if you don't feel like community service is in your DNA, it's something worth considering as you head into adulthood: It makes the world a better place to live, and research has found that performing acts of kindness is highly correlated with a boost in happiness and improves both our sense of self-image and our sense of community.

Don't Know How to Start Giving Back? Try This

Google for good.

Review your values and pick a goal: If you could change anything about the state of the world or your community, what would it be? Search online for those keywords and your city and state. You'll find plenty of opportunities to get involved.

Make it a social event.

Do your friends do any volunteer work? If so, join them to see whether you'd enjoy it. If not, invite your friends along to an activity that you've found: Getting friends in the act makes your contributions that much

"Together We Can Create a More Peaceful Future": A WTF Story of Community Engagement

"As a junior in high school I was given the opportunity to watch a documentary called 'Invisible Children' for extra credit. I am not someone who is naturally inclined to take any available opportunity for extra points, but I was not doing very well in the class at the time and decided to do what I could to boost my grade. Instead of attending a community screening, I opted to watch the documentary the night before the assignment was due on Google Video. The film only lasted fifty minutes, but by the end I had been jarred from my state of apathy. It was not the heart-wrenching stories of suffering depicted in the documentary that moved me, but the fact that the film established a personal connection between me and youth affected by war in northern Uganda. The feeling of personal connection enlightened me to the agency each of us has to make a positive impact on the lives of others.

"Two years later I entered college at a moment of possibility in the fall of 2008, and was caught up in the environment of optimism that enveloped much of the millennial generation. As a result, a group of friends and I decided to start an organization called One Life One World One Peace on campus with the mission of using technology to establish connections between youth around the world and having those relationships act as inspiration to address the root causes of conflicts. The idea exploded in our imaginations and I soon found myself filling out paperwork to register the group as a nonprofit organization.

"The process of starting the organization has not been linear. We have had to refine our ideas and find ways to turn them into

→

> tangible forms of action. At the same time, everyone in the organization is a full-time student and has to contend with many competing interests. Yet I continue to work on making the vision of One Life a reality because of the possibility that together we can create a more peaceful future and out of a fierce urgency to act that is gained through associations with others."
>
> —Eric, founder of One Life One World One Peace
>
> www.1life1world1peace.org

more meaningful and increases the fun. Plus, you'll encourage each other to continue after that first week.

Pick an activity where you'll see results quickly.

If you're on the fence about whether service work makes a difference, try something that will pay dividends sooner rather than later. Think community gardening, a neighborhood cleanup, or helping kids with their homework.

Be open to receive—and give.

Generosity makes you feel good. And, as Suze Orman writes in her bestseller, *The 9 Steps to Financial Freedom*, if you think about money not from an accumulation perspective, but from a giving perspective, you're more likely to realize the abundance of gifts that you've been given. "If we are grasping what we have so tightly, we are not open to receive or even notice all that may be trying to flow our way," she writes.

Embrace Your Jen

In his 2009 book, *Born to Be Good: The Science of a Meaningful Life*, psychology professor Dacher Keltner argues that humans are hardwired for kindness, not evil. He introduces readers to the Confucian teaching of *jen*— "a complex mixture of kindness, humanity, and respect that transpires between people." A person of *jen*, according to Confucius, is someone who leads by example—and you can feel jen in that "deeply satisfying moment when you bring out the goodness in others." Indeed, we are wired for jen, he argues. When we volunteer, act kindly, or give of ourselves, our brain lights up in ways that give us particular pleasure.

Engage in five acts of kindness in a week. Hold the door open for someone behind you, even if it means you have to stop for a second to wait. Give money to someone in need. Donate blood. Write a note to your parents telling them how much you appreciate their support. Volunteer. It will boost your happiness and well-being considerably.

Maybe you've never donated to charity because you feel like you're broke. In the future, when you get rich, you'll donate, right? Well, Orman's chapters on generosity helped many WTFers start thinking in new ways about giving back.

Open Your Hands

Try this, Orman says: Turn on the faucet in your kitchen. Make a tight fist with both hands and try to get enough water from that faucet to get a real drink from your fists. It doesn't work. "Now open up your hands, cup them. Put them under the faucet and accept the water flowing freely into your hands. You'll be able to drink to your heart's content."

The message is clear. It works the same way with our money and time: If we're grasping at things so tightly, we aren't able to receive all the joy that life has to offer.

To open up their hands, WTF testers said they got involved with volunteer activities and charities—and were amazed. When some friends organized a breast cancer awareness hockey tournament, Sam both donated money and volunteered her time. She also participated in the dance marathon to raise money for the local children's hospital. "Even though my addition to these organizations was not much, it made me see that if I just looked at my money differently, then I can open myself up to being able to have money to do things for other people without having to take away from other necessities. I may not be a wife or a mom yet, but being able to make myself do that kind of planning has shown me that I will be able to manage my money when the time comes for me to have to do it on my own."

Open Your Mind

Volunteering isn't about talking down to people—it's about expressing honest interest, and that's something that Dale Carnegie's *How to Win Friends and Influence People* really reminded WTF testers.

Small Donations Can Make a Big Difference

Every month, make a donation to an organization of your choosing. It doesn't have to be a big gift—just something small to do your part. Victoria said she tried this and "it makes me feel worthier and full of grace. I think this is an incredibly important thing to do even if many people don't realize it at first."

John used Carnegie's advice to express honest interest with one of the women in the special-needs facility where he volunteers. Vickie would often complain that she was still hungry after the meal was served and asked for seconds repeatedly. John would usually dismiss her with a comment about how it's against the rules and walk away so as to avoid her frustration. "After reading Carnegie's advice I decided that I was going to attempt to deal with her in a more sincere fashion," John said.

"On one particular evening, a nurse's aide brought her to the dining room a little early. I approached her and asked if I could visit with her for a moment. Immediately she asked if there was anything she could snack on. I explained to her that, though personally I didn't mind, I had been under a lot of heat from my new boss to follow procedure. She replied that she understood and then asked if I was a student and what it was that I was studying. When I told her that I was a psychology major with an interest in pursuing a master's in social work, Vickie's eyes lit up. She explained that before her accident she had been a counseling social worker specializing in child therapy. It was from that moment forward that a bond formed between us, leading to many interesting conversations about the different types of therapy and some of the experiences that she has had."

Now, John said, she's in a better mood when he works at the clinic—and Vickie repaid his kindness by complimenting his already noticeable therapeutic skills. "She told me I'll make a good therapist one day, and that really meant a lot to me."

To be truly wise, tenacious, and fearless means getting outside yourself and building healthy, loving relationships with others. So set some goals here: What step might you take in the next week to build a better relationship with your family, with a friend or significant other, and with your community? Write it down here and make a commitment to get out there and be fearless.

In the next week, I will strengthen the relationship with my family by:

_____

In the next week, I will strengthen the relationship with my friend or significant other by:

_____

In the next week, I will strengthen the relationship with my neighbors and community by:

_____

Share Your Blessings: A WTF Volunteer Story

"I was lucky enough to grow up with an enthusiastic mother and a positive older sister who always encouraged me to pursue my education, especially after high school. I turned to my older sister when it came to advice about boys, rumors, or other friendship problems. My teenage mind thought, 'She is not much older than me so I bet she'll know what to do.' This is ultimately what I want to give back to young students now: My goal is to encourage and advise.

"Unfortunately, not all children have the positive influence that

→

←

I was so blessed with. I watched as some of my friends in high school floundered in confusion when it came to college because many of their parents had never attended college. I don't think it is fair that completely capable and hardworking kids should miss out on higher education simply because they didn't know much about preparing, searching, or applying to college.

"I became involved with a mentoring program my sophomore year through the National Society of Collegiate Scholars and began tutoring at local middle schools and high schools. College students working with kids can provide a clear, positive example of what the younger students can aspire to be. By building strong relationships, the kids can feel open to talk to their mentors about subjects other than math, science, or college prep, such as real-life issues. One positive role model in the life of a child can make a huge difference.

"It's not always easy, but it has been extremely rewarding: I juggled work, school, friends, and being in a serious relationship to make time to tutor, so I can understand when people think that they don't have the time. However, take it from me: It is very possible with simple time-management skills. Plan ahead when you will study and stay committed. Watch TV two nights a week instead of five. One or two hours a week spent with younger students who look forward to spending time with a 'cool college student' will not be the straw that breaks the camel's back. Simply hanging out, studying, laughing, and listening with these developing minds is both fun and satisfying."

—Derilyn, a volunteer for the National Society
of Collegiate Scholars

WTF Did I Just Learn?

Congratulations! You completed the third stage of the WTF transformation. If you learned about your money psychology, if you made some commitments to get thrifty, if you learned how to interview like a pro and how to become more involved with your community, and if you're excited to apply this knowledge to your life . . . *you just got Fearless!*

Here's a quick review:

Thrift: Thrift isn't about being stingy, it's about understanding the right use of money, time, and energy to thrive in your life. If you know where your money goes each week and each month, you can ask yourself if your spending is in line with your goals, values, and personal mission statement.

Smile: Many WTFers are in the job market, trying to ace their next interview to move ahead on a career path. Smiling, admitting your mistakes, and thinking in terms of benefits for everyone makes your work life—and life in general—go more smoothly.

Make meaning: A lot of us are pretty self-absorbed. But to make meaning in your life and truly boost your overall happiness means investing in more meaningful friendships, relationships, and community outreach. To be truly fearless, WTFers need to get outside themselves—and this chapter provided you with dozens of suggestions for how to think outside the "you" box in your own life.

Questions to ask yourself:

- ▶ Where does my money go? Is my *spending in line with my values?*
- ▶ What specific steps can I take to *save money*—and prioritize important purchases?
- ▶ How can I *think win/win* in my personal and professional life?
- ▶ How can I *be more present* in my conversations with friends?
- ▶ What are some ways I can *improve my relationships* with loved ones?
- ▶ In the next week, what one step will I take to *get more involved in my community?*
- ▶ Have I really committed to becoming fearless in my financial, personal and professional life?

If you haven't committed to trying at least one of these areas of change, go back to pages 158–61 and fill out the "WTF Does My Money Go?" worksheet: *Only you can give yourself a gold star for being Fearless.*

Generation WTF

Five Things to Do before You Put This Book Away

You are Generation WTF—a wise, tenacious, and fearless group of young adults that can make a difference in the world. Becoming **Wise** means figuring out who you are and where your strengths should guide you. Becoming **Tenacious** means mastering your time and focusing your energy. Becoming **Fearless** is all about understanding how you can best interact with the world around you. But you're not finished yet: **Being a proud member of Generation WTF means living out these lessons on a daily basis.**

Why?

Because to thrive—to have a deep sense of personal wellbeing— means to excel at these skills of wisdom, tenacity, and fearlessness every day. It's not easy, but it's certainly possible.

According to hundreds of small- and large-scale Gallup opinion polls, empirical studies, and time-use data collected over the last few years, wellbeing isn't just about some amorphous sense of being happy. It's about thriving in career, social, financial, physical, and community life, areas that we've covered in this book.

In their 2010 book *Wellbeing: The Five Essential Elements*, authors Tom Rath and Jim Harter describe ultimate wellbeing as follows:

► **Career Wellbeing:** According to decades of research, liking what you do for work—whether it's paid or unpaid, at home or in an office—is one of the primary determinants of your overall wellbeing. If you like your job, you're twice as likely to be thriving in your overall life. People who like what they do are sick less often, feel like the day goes by faster, and are more engaged in other aspects of their personal lives, too. If you are disengaged at work, you're more likely to suffer from depression in the next year.

→ **Want to find the best career for you?** Review chapter 1 to vocalize your purpose and chapter 7 to land the job with great interpersonal skills.

► **Social Wellbeing:** On average, you need six hours of social time to have a "thriving" day—defined as a day that you'd like to repeat again in the future. This social time can be combined with attention to your physical wellbeing or your career wellbeing, of course: You get double the happiness boost from going on a run with a buddy and having a best friend at your office. But don't think that one best friend is going to be your everything. Share the love.

→ **Want to strengthen your social life?** Take the time-chart challenge in chapter 2, review chapter 5 to stop procrastinating, and embrace chapter 8 to make your relationships more meaningful.

► **Financial Wellbeing:** While money doesn't buy happiness, it certainly helps. On the whole, people who live in more affluent countries are more likely to be thriving. Still, it's your sense of financial security—not your income—that has the most substantial impact on your overall wellbeing: Someone who has a more moderate income but doesn't worry about money so much is going to be happier than that person's rich, but anxious, neighbor. And if you've got money to spend, splurge on experiences rather than things for maximum wellbeing bang for your buck.

→ **Want to be thrifty and still thrive?** Review chapter 6 to figure out where your money really goes and be sure your spending is in line with your values.

▶ **Physical Wellbeing:** Exercise, sleep, and good personal health are crucial to thrive in your overall life. Exercise reduces fatigue, a good night's sleep is nature's reset button, and educated choices about the food you eat today helps you feel better tomorrow. Set up default strategies to help your health—like going to a restaurant that serves only salads, rather than asking yourself to pass up a burger once the menu and smells are messing with your self-control—and you'll be more likely to succeed. Psychological research backs this up, too.

→ **Want to get in better shape?** You *do* have time to exercise, as you'll see in the chapter 2 time-chart challenge. Plus, by reviewing the basics of diet and self-control in chapter 4, you'll be on track to a healthier you in no time.

▶ **Community Wellbeing:** This is the difference between a good life and a great life, but it's an area many of us struggle: We're so wrapped up in our own problems we don't get out of ourselves and join community groups, spiritual support networks, and volunteer organizations nearly as much as we should to maximize our overall wellbeing. Think about your passions and your personal gifts, and then figure out some small way that you could be useful to others.

→ **Want to get more involved?** Use chapter 1 to figure out how your personal talents can be useful to the community and review chapter 8 for inspirational stories about how WTFers like you have made a difference.

So What Next?

You've built up a lot of momentum as you read this book. You're feeling empowered and organized. Don't lose that feeling! Before you put this book away, finalize your personal mission statement, get online to find more interactive tools, and post your core values front and center. Then, set a goal to achieve in the next week and tell at least one other person about the progress you've made.

1. Finalize Your Personal Mission Statement

In chapter 1 you began outlining your personal mission statement. Maybe you even drafted it. Look back over your notes and finalize your personal constitution. Go online to read the mission statements of others for more ideas. But don't put this book down without completing this exercise.

Complete these sentences to help you get started. And then write away.

I will be a _____.

I will strive to _____.

I will stand for _____.

I will be remembered for _____.

Special Online Bonus

After you've written your personal mission statement, make sure you'll be reminded of it in the future. Go to www.generationwtf.com to find out more.

2. Join the Generation WTF Movement

Go online to www.generationwtf.com right now. Sign up for e-mail updates, interactive online-only features, and a community of like-minded peers. Yes, you've finished the book, but making these changes stick means living out the recommendations on a day-to-day basis. Behavioral change takes a village, and you can find yours at www.generationwtf.com.

3. Remember Your Core Values

Write down your five core values and stick them on your computer, in your wallet, or on the bathroom mirror—anywhere that you'll see them often.

Copy the template on the next page, or go to www.generationwtf.com to print one out.

My Five Core Values Are

1. _____

2. _____

3. _____

4. _____

5. _____

4. Set a Goal—and Accomplish It—This Week

Pick a goal and set out to achieve it the SMARTER way by the end of the week. Got so many you don't know where to start? Try setting a thrift goal first. Figure out where your money goes and how you can better tailor your spending to your values. Giving back to your family, friends, or community would be an excellent place to start as well. But pick something that you are passionate about—right now—and stick to it.

Want to be reminded of your goal? Go online to www.generationwtf .com to sign up to receive e-mail reminders of your goals in the coming weeks and months.

5. Spread the News

Research finds that public commitments to change are a lot more likely to "stick" than private commitments to change, so pick at least one person and tell him or her about your work with this book. Talk about your commitments to personal improvement and the goals you've set along the way.

This book isn't meant to be read and then put away to gather dust: It's an action book that can be used whenever you've got a big project or deadline coming up, and whenever you need a brushup on some people skills to get you where you want to go.

Tell friends about the skills you've learned and encourage them to try them out, too. Self-control is "contagious," so if your friends get on board for a wise, tenacious, and fearless existence, you are all on the road to success.

Generation WTF has seen some tough times recently, there's no

Generation WTF Advice:
After Reading the Advice of Others,
Your Peers Offered Some of Their Own

- ▶ Don't be afraid to say "no," even if your friends don't like you for it!
- ▶ Be thrifty: Spend time and money wisely.
- ▶ If you have self-control, everything else will be a lot easier.
- ▶ Always meet with your professor at least once.
- ▶ Don't tell lies about the way you feel. Speak the truth as you understand it.
- ▶ Don't blow your money on booze.
- ▶ Learn the value of perseverance and hard work.
- ▶ Ask questions if you don't understand something.
- ▶ It is not a bad thing to go wild at some point. Just learn from your mistakes and learn moderation.
- ▶ Appreciate and treat your parents well. Keep developing that relationship.
- ▶ If your first test is bad, just remember there will be a second.
- ▶ If you do not go out tonight, I guarantee people will go out tomorrow (you aren't missing anything).
- ▶ Face adversity head-on.
- ▶ Put the pain before the pleasure.
- ▶ Get involved in all different types of activities.
- ▶ It's better to be late to class than not go at all.
- ▶ Learn how to have fun without drinking.

→

> ←
> ▶ Perseverance, thrift, honesty, and self-control: Combine them for the most success. And don't try things alone: Let people know you are doing something to change so they can help you.
> ▶ Set some money aside for fun extras: You're only young once.
> ▶ Call home at least every few days.
> ▶ If you disagree, do it in a calm controlled manner, and if you're wrong, admit it.
> ▶ Experience all you can.
> ▶ Think of life like a cake: Delay the frosting as long as possible. It tastes better that way and it usually means more good stuff.

denying it. Yet through the wisdom of old-school self-help made new and applicable for twenty-first-century success, you have learned how to be **Wise**—and embrace the "I" in your statements of purpose. You have learned to be **Tenacious** and focused on accomplishing your goals. And now it's time to be **Fearless** and take these skills off the pages and into your bright future.

I believe in you. And as you come to these final pages, I can hear a resounding chorus from Generation WTF worldwide: We can change that term of exasperation into one of empowerment. We can turn that acronym of frustration into one of freedom. We can be a wise, tenacious, and fearless generation.

Yes we can!

Acknowledgements

Generation WTF is dedicated to my students at the University of Iowa and the University of Pittsburgh—the Generation WTF testers who trusted me enough to live the advice in dozens of self-help manuals and share their personal experiences along the way. You are a wise, tenacious, and fearless inspiration to us all.

Special thanks to Michael Leytem and Erin Wagoner, who were both my students and research assistants in the two years I worked on this project. Thanks also to undergraduate teaching assistants Taryn Deutsch and Aaron Vincent for making the project more manageable.

This book began as an academic exploration of the impact of old-school self-help advice on Millennial young adults. But with the guidance of Susan Arellano, Natalie Silver, and the enthusiastic young minds at Templeton Press, it has blossomed into so much more. My sincere thanks to Templeton Press for allowing me the time to get it right and to Dr. John Templeton for believing in the project from the start.

Academic research, no matter how popular the final result, relies on the expertise of others. There aren't many of us who study the self-help industry with such vigor, and I offer thanks to Micki McGee, Steve Salerno, and Martin Seligman for their insights into the business of self-improvement. In addition, my colleagues at the University of

Iowa kept me on track and focused: Many thanks to Celesta Albonetti, Alison Bianchi, Christie Boxer, Mary Campbell, Philip Deslippe, Ben Earnhart, Jennifer Glanville, Steve Hitlin, Mary Noonan, Jenn Turchi, Valentino Russell, and Susannah Wood. Many thanks also to the professors and graduate students at the University of Pittsburgh who supported me through the final stages of this book.

I'm blessed with a terrific community of writers and friends who have offered specific input along the way: Thanks to Elissa Ashwood, David Kahn, Nic Kelman, Bill McGarvey, Naomi Schaefer Riley, David Robinson, Phil Fox Rose, Alexcis Reynolds, David Smith, Gladys Stone, Laura Vanderkam, and Fred Whelan.

I'll forever be indebted to my academic—and life—advisors, Don Drakeman and Avner Offer, for their support in my education, academic, and writing careers. You both knew a book like this was coming well before I did.

None of this would be possible without the support of my loving family: My parents, Elizabeth and Stephen Whelan, my parents-in-law, Katherine and John Moyers and my in-laws, Anna and Jeff Stone, who patiently supported me every step of the way.

And most importantly, a loving thank-you to my husband, Peter. We're a wise, tenacious, and fearless team, and I couldn't have done it without you.

A WTF Advanced Calendar Strategy to Keep You on Track

You've set out your goals the SMARTER way in chapter 3, and now you're looking to stay on track. When a big project is looming, here's your step-by-step plan to the "T"—tracking—in the SMARTER strategy.

1. **Get out a calendar.** (You can download a template on www.generationwtf.com)

2. **Set your ultimate deadline**—perhaps something like "Project Due to Boss on January 20."

3. It's early November, and that project deadline seems eons away. But what specific steps do you need to take to accomplish it? **Break it into at least five steps**—probably more.

4. Then, working backwards, **figure out deadlines for each individual step**.

5. To follow along and do this for your own project, **go to www.generationwtf.com to print your own calendar**.

Here's how I created this sample calendar:

It's early November and I've procrastinated on my term paper for graduate school. It's due in mid-January, when everyone returns from the winter holiday—but there are plenty of other things I want to be doing during those months, too.

November 2011

October 2011	November 2011	December 2011
S M T W T F S	S M T W T F S	S M T W T F S
1	1 2 3 4 5	1 2 3
2 3 4 5 6 7 8	6 7 8 9 10 11 12	4 5 6 7 8 9 10
9 10 11 12 13 14 15	13 14 15 16 17 18 19	11 12 13 14 15 16 17
16 17 18 19 20 21 22	20 21 22 23 24 25 26	18 19 20 21 22 23 24
23 24 25 26 27 28 29	27 28 29 30	25 26 27 28 29 30 31
30 31		

Sunday	Monday	Tuesday	Wednesday	Thursday	Friday	Saturday
6	7	1	2	3	4	5
13	7 1	8 research history section	9	10	11	12
20	2	15 write history section	16	17	18	19
27	21 buffer day	22 day to prepare	23 home for thanksgiving	24	25	26
	28 day to refocus	29 3	30 research women			

December 2011

Sunday	Monday	Tuesday	Wednesday	Thursday	Friday	Saturday
4	5 4	6 write what women want	7	1	2	3
11	12 5	13 research men	14	8	9	10
18	19 6	20 start/finish writing what men want	21	15 day to prepare	16 start writing men section	17
25 travel	26 w/family	27	28 probably not working	22	23 holiday	24
				29	30 new year's eve w/friends	31

January 2012

	December 2011	January 2012	February 2012
	S M T W T F S	S M T W T F S	S M T W T F S
	1 2 3	1 2 3 4 5 6 7	1 2 3 4
	4 5 6 7 8 9 10	8 9 10 11 12 13 14	5 6 7 8 9 10 11
	11 12 13 14 15 16 17	15 16 17 18 19 20 21	12 13 14 15 16 17 18
	18 19 20 21 22 23 24	22 23 24 25 26 27 28	19 20 21 22 23 24 25
	25 26 27 28 29 30 31	29 30 31	26 27 28

Sunday	Monday	Tuesday	Wednesday	Thursday	Friday	Saturday
1	2	3	4	5	6	7
8	9	10 finish men section	11 write intro	12	13	14
15 my → deadline	16 9 *	17 write conclusion	18	19 footnotes and citations	20 DUE!	21
22	23	24	25	26	27	28
29	30	31				

Topic =   Paper on Changing Dating and Marriage Patterns in the U.S.

Deadline =   Jan. 20

It's going to be a thirty-page paper with three sections. I'll need to do research for each, outline each, and then write it. There will also need to be an introduction and conclusion. Oh, and my least favorite thing: footnotes and citations.

That means I should break the project down into five big steps:

Section 1: History

Section 2: What Women Want

Section 3: What Men Want

Introduction and Conclusion

Footnotes and Citations

Initially, I decided it would take me two weeks for each part—two weeks to research, outline, and write each section, two weeks for the intro and conclusion, and then two weeks to deal with all the final bits.

Be Honest about Your Commitments When Scheduling

This is a very important part of the scheduling process: Be honest about when you will and won't work. Build in a buffer, too, because life doesn't always go according to plan. Even if you work at a "real job" and have to go to the office on those days, some days more is going to get done than others. You might have 150 e-mails to catch up on. You might just be too exhausted to function at 100 percent. We're being real in this schedule so we don't run out of time later on.

That seemed great, because the deadline was eleven weeks away.

But then I looked at the calendar—Thanksgiving, Christmas, and New Year's all fall during my project timeline.

So I blocked out those days in the calendar. But then, to be reasonable, I also blocked out the day before and after I planned to travel—because, let's be honest, I've got to pack, get gifts, and generally get my life together. No work would get done.

That leaves me with nine weeks—well, really, eight-and-a-half—to work with.

I can do the footnotes and citations in one week if I'm good about taking notes as I research. I can probably even write the intro and conclusion in a week(ish). But what I must not sacrifice is the final few days as a buffer to pull it all together.

I make my personal deadline January 16—four days before the project is due—giving me time to do last-minute changes, or to scramble if I get off schedule. So now we're down to fewer than eight weeks.

And yes, at that point I'm a bit panicked. But that's the idea—better now than later.

Week 1: I research the history section.

Week 2: I write the history section.

Week 3: I research what women want.

Week 4: I write the "what women want" section.

All sounds good . . . but then the pace picks up quickly. I can assume that after researching and writing two sections I've gotten the hang of the project, so I've left less time to complete the third section. Risky? Yep. But nothing like a deadline to motivate you to work during the weekends, too.

Week 5: I research what men want—and start writing the "what men want" section.

Week 6: I commit to finishing the "what men want" section before leaving for Christmas.

Week 7: It's a new year, and there's lots of work to do. I finish any leftover work there is to do on the previous sections and start in on the introduction.

Week 8: I write the conclusion—and do as good of a job as I can muster on footnotes and citations in the final few days.

But wait . . . if I really meet all these deadlines, I now have four more days to fix the footnotes, review the manuscript as a whole, and create a polished product.

Victory: More Helpful Tips

Build in a buffer. If a project is due to your boss June 1, aim to have it totally completed by May 15. This leaves you a few weeks to polish it up, or, more likely, gives you a buffer in case your best-laid plans go awry.

Be honest about your other commitments. Big holiday weeks, vacations, visits from friends and family are *not* the times when you are going to be most productive. So plan accordingly: If your five closest friends are coming for the weekend, set a deadline for a few days *before* they arrive, and another deadline for a reasonable amount of time after they leave.

Don't panic if, as you're working backward, you run out of time. That's the whole point of the exercise. Just reconfigure the plan, and remember, you don't have as much time as you think.

Bad at sticking to deadlines? Add incentives—or other binding commitments—to spur you along. I spent the last year of my doctoral studies in New York, while my advisor was back in Oxford, England.

That meant that I had to fly to England a few times a year to meet with him to go over my chapter drafts and discuss the progress of my research. So, I'd plan out when each chapter had to be e-mailed to him, and I'd buy the cheapest, *nonrefundable* plane tickets I could find for two weeks later. I had to get the material to my advisor with enough time for him to read it and offer comments; otherwise I would be throwing away my money on a plane ticket for a visit that wouldn't benefit my research. Needless to say, I never missed a deadline with that self-imposed evil strategy!

Try it for yourself by going to www.generationwtf.com and printing out your sample planner.

Notes

Introduction

2 *But if you're like most of Generation WTF* . . . Emily Nussbaum, *New York Magazine,* June 7 2009, http://nymag.com/news/features/57204/.

4 *The average college graduate will leave school* . . . "Data Shows Students Charge Average of $2,200 in Direct Education Expenses," Sallie Mae, April 13, 2009, http://www.salliemae.com/about/news_info/newsreleases/041309.htm.

4 *In May 2009, as college seniors graduated* . . . National Association of Colleges and Employers, 2009, http://ww.naceweb.org/Research/Job_Outlook/Purchase_Job_Outlook_2009.aspx.

4 *By 2010 the job market was picking up a bit* . . . National Association of Colleges and Employers Job Outlook 2010, Spring Update, http://www.naceweb.org/Publications/Spotlight_Online/2010/0414/Job_Outlook_Hiring_Up_5_3_Percent_for_Class_of_2010.aspx.

1. Who Are You?

16 *"Trust me, the Value Circle™ exercise* . . . David Bach, *The Finish Rich Workbook* (New York: Broadway Books, 2003), 29.

21 *An ongoing study of young adults.* . . William Damon, *The Path to Purpose* (New York: Free Press, 2008).

23 *It turns out that one of the prime predictors* . . . Damon, *The Path to Purpose,* 26.

23 *"Noble purpose can be found* . . . Damon, *The Path to Purpose,* 44.

24 *And when you do that, studies find* . . . M. C. Wittrock, "Generative Learning Processes of the Brain," *Educational Psychologist* 27, no. 4 (1992): 531–41.

24 *Those are great goals—and do give many people purpose* . . . Damon, *The Path to Purpose,* 28.

28 *This statement should be the "basis for making daily decisions* . . . Stephen Covey, *The 7 Habits of Highly Effective People* (1989; repr., New York: Fireside, 1990 edition), 108.

29 *Your mission statement will guide you* . . . Covey, *The 7 Habits of Highly Effective People*, 107, 108.

2. Get Honest with Yourself

36 *From spiritual practices to psychotherapy* . . . Christopher Peterson and Martin Seligman, *Character Strengths and Virtues: A Handbook and Classification* (New York: Oxford University Press, 2004), 268.

39 *One study suggests that the average person* . . . *Daily Mail*, 2008 survey, http://www.wnd.com/?pageId=45642, and "Men Lie Six Times a Day and Twice as Often as Women, Study Finds," *Daily Mail*, September 14, 2009, http://www.dailymail.co.uk/news/article-1213171/Men-lie-times-day-twice-women-study-finds.html.

41 *But studies show vegging out* . . . Bruno S. Frey, Christine Benesch, and Alois Stutzer, "Does Watching TV Make Us Happy?" *Journal of Economic Psychology* 28, no. 3 (2007): 283–313.

43 *He suggests starting a confidential journal* . . . Phil McGraw, *Life Strategies* (New York: Hyperion, 1999) 19, 29, 53, 180.

44 *If you hope to have a winning life strategy* . . . McGraw, *Life Strategies*, 110, 199.

44 *Your life is not too bad to fix* . . . McGraw, *Life Strategies*, 118–19.

45 *What does seem to make people happy* . . . Richard Wiseman, *59 Seconds: Think a Little, Change a Lot* (New York: Knopf, 2009).

45 *Keeping a gratitude journal encourages people* . . . For a list of dozens of gratitude research citations, visit http://psychology.ucdavis.edu/labs/emmons/.

45 *For five days, write about* . . . Wiseman, *59 Seconds*, 23–25.

48 *face up to what you are really doing with your money* . . . Suze Orman, *The 9 Steps to Financial Freedom* (1997; repr. New York: Three Rivers Press, 2000), 36.

49 *Of course, researchers had passed off a ten-dollar Cabernet Sauvignon* . . . Hilke Plassmann, John O'Doherty, Baba Shiv, and Antonio Rangel, "Marketing Actions Can Modulate Neural Representations of Experienced Pleasantness," *Proceedings of the National Academy of Sciences*, 105, no. 3 (January 22, 2008): 1050–54. Also, see the article about it here: http://dsc.discovery.com/news/2008/01/14/wine-brain-behavior.html.

3. Got Goal?

57 *Or, think of it another way* . . . Stephen Covey, *The 7 Habits of Highly Effective People* (1989; repr., New York: Fireside, 1990 edition), 147, 149, 169.

58 *Since the 1960s, researchers* . . . For more information, see the work of Prof. Edwin A. Locke on goal-setting theory.

58 *One of the most popular goal-setting acronyms* . . . No one really knows where this

acronym first began, but self-help books have embraced it. The earliest known site is George T. Doran, "There's a S.M.A.R.T. Way to Write Management's Goals and Objectives," *Management Review* 70, no. 11 (November 1981). For more on this mnemonic: http://www.rapidbi.com/created/WriteSMARTobjectives.html.

59 *And that is perseverance and tenacity in the practical sense* . . . Christopher Peterson and Martin Seligman, *Character Strengths and Virtues: A Handbook and Classification* (New York: Oxford University Press, 2004), 229.

59 *Just thinking about a goal isn't perseverance* . . . Peterson and Seligman, *Character Strengths and Virtues*, 230.

60 *Write down a specific goal* . . . For more information, see the academic work of Albert Bandura. Goal specificity, goal challenge, and goal proximity are all factors of motivation to change, Bandura finds. Personal incentives increase when the goal is specific so that accomplishments are unambiguous. Interest and involvement are sparked by challenge. And for long-term goals, people need immediate steps, or subgoals, to achieve; otherwise they will put off their efforts. Writing a satisfactory doctoral dissertation yields an advanced degree, a specific goal that is quite challenging. To finish the doctoral dissertation takes years, and outlines; small deadlines and daily goals are helpful to achieve the goal over time. As this process proves, a person's self-efficacy increases when small goals are set and achieved regularly.

60 *When it's clear what we need* . . . A. Bandura, *Self-Efficacy: The Exercise of Control* (New York: Worth Publishers, 1997), 133–35.

61 *To achieve a long-term goal* . . . Bandura, *Self-Efficacy*.

61 *By breaking down a goal* . . . Richard Wiseman, 59 *Seconds: Think a Little, Change a Lot* (New York: Knopf, 2009), 85.

62 *For each step, ask yourself* . . . See Bandura, Wiseman, and others.

63 *Believing you are capable of success* . . . Bandura, *Self-Efficacy*.

64 *Bonus: Researchers have found that people* . . . http://citeseerx.ist.psu.edu/viewdoc/download?doi=10.1.1.127.5140&rep=rep1&type=pdf.

65 *British author Samuel Smiles* . . . Note: The second edition of *Self-Help*, in 1866, added "Perseverance" to the subtitle.

65 *To expand the audience of his advice* . . . Smiles, *Self-Help*, 12, 13.

66 *"When I returned* . . . Samuel Smiles, *Self-Help*, ed. Ralph Lytton Bower (New York: American Book Co., 1904), 82.

68 *From a mid-century longitudinal study* . . . L. M. Terman and M. H. Oden, *Genetic Studies of Genius: Vol. 4. The Gifted Child Grows Up* (Palo Alto, CA: Stanford University Press, 1947), 351; Duckworth and Peterson, "Grit: Perseverance and Passion for Long-Term Goals" (2007), 1.

68 *A now-classic study of violinists* . . . K. A. Ericsson and N. Charness, "Expert Performance: Its Structure and Acquisition," *American Psychologist* 49 (1994): 725–47.

69   *Physical, social/emotional, mental, and spiritual renewal* . . . Covey, *The 7 Habits of Highly Effective People*, 228.

69   *Indeed, psychologist Richard Wiseman found that* . . . Wiseman, *59 Seconds*, 86–87.

73   *"We think of effortless performance* . . . M. S. Peck, *The Road Less Traveled: A New Psychology of Love, Traditional Values and Spiritual Growth* (New York: Simon & Schuster, 1978), 19.

4. Self-Control

81   *"It's much more important than that* . . . Jonah Lehrer, "Don't," *New Yorker*, May 18, 2009.

81   *Pretending that the candy isn't real* . . . Lehrer, "Don't."

82   *The formal, academic definition* . . . C. E. Thoresen and M. J. Mahoney, *Behavioral Self-Control* (New York: Holt, Rinehart, & Winston, 1974), 2, 9, and 12.

82   *"If you do that, you're in control* . . . A. Robbins, *Awaken the Giant Within: How to Take Immediate Control of Your Mental, Emotional, Physical and Financial Destiny* (New York: Free Press, 1991), 54.

83   *Real personal control means saying no* . . . For the meatier arguments behind these ideas, see W. Mischel et al., "Sustaining Delay of Gratification over Time: A Hot-Cold Systems Perspective," and T. O'Donoghue and M. Rabin, "Self-Awareness and Self-Control," both in *Time and Decision: Economic and Psychological Perspectives on Intertemporal Choice*, ed. G. Loewenstein, D. Read, and R. Baumeister (New York: Russell Sage Foundation, 2003), 175 and 222 respectively.

83   *This, of course, makes self-control harder to keep up* . . . For a more academic treatment of this idea, see G. Loewenstein and R. H. Thaler, "Anomalies: Intertemporal Choice," *Journal of Economic Perspectives* 3, no. 4 (1989): 181; G. Ainslie, *Breakdown of Will* (Cambridge: Cambridge University Press, 2001), 47.

84   *Just like feeling out of control of your life* . . . A. Bandura, *Self-Efficacy: The Exercise of Control* (New York: Worth Publishers, 1997), 159.

84   *To understand that life is a skill* . . . Phil McGraw, *Life Strategies* (New York: Hyperion, 1999), 38.

85   *"Our behavior is a function of our decisions* . . . Stephen Covey, *The 7 Habits of Highly Effective People*, (1989; repr., New York: Fireside, 1990 edition), 71.

85   *A reactive person says* . . . Covey, *The 7 Habits of Highly Effective People*, 77.

85   *And while we can't control the world* . . . Covey, *The 7 Habits of Highly Effective People*, 81–83.

88   *Character is primary, personality is secondary* . . . Covey, *The 7 Habits of Highly Effective People*, 18, 23–27.

88   *Rather than superficial changes* . . . Covey, *The 7 Habits of Highly Effective People*, 42.

89 *On the first reading, Covey suggests readers engage* . . . Covey, *The 7 Habits of Highly Effective People*, 60.

92 *"Some people say that you* . . . Covey, *The 7 Habits of Highly Effective People*, 186.

92 *"make a promise—and keep it* . . . Covey, *The 7 Habits of Highly Effective People*, 92.

95 *People who believe they can change* . . . J. R. Schallow, "Locus of Control and Success at Self-Modification," *Behavior Therapy* 6 (1975): 669; and R. R. McCrae and J. Paul T. Costa, "Personality, Coping, and Coping Effectiveness in an Adult Sample," *Journal of Personality* 54, no. 2 (1986): 385–405.

95 *Self-esteem is about judgments of self-worth* . . . Bandura, *Self-Efficacy*, 11.

98 *If a dog is tired* . . . Holly C. Miller, Kristina F. Pattison, C. Nathan DeWall, Rebecca Rayburn-Reeves, and Thomas R. Zentall, "Self-Control Without a 'Self'? Common Self-Control Processes in Humans and Dogs," *Psychological Science* 21 (April 2010): 534–38, first published on March 11, 2010 (abstract at: http://pss.sagepub.com/content/early/2010/03/11/0956797610364968.abstract).

98 *Just like you're not going to have your best workout* . . . R. Baumeister and K. D. Vohs, "Willpower, Choice, and Self-Control," in *Time and Decision*, ed. Loewenstein, Read, and Baumeister, 214; and R. Baumeister and T. F. Heatherton, "Self-Regulation Failure: An Overview," *Psychological Inquiry* 7, no. 1 (1996): 3.

100 *In a 1980s study* . . . Brownell, Heckerman, Westlake, Hayes, and Monti (1978), as quoted in G. M. Rosen and R. E. Glasgow, "Self-Help Behavior Therapy Manuals: Recent Developments and Clinical Usage," in *New Developments in Behavior Therapy: From Research to Clinical Application*, ed. C. Franks (New York: Routledge, 1984), 536.

101 *AA tells recovering alcoholics* . . . Ainslie, *Breakdown of Will*, 97.

101 *Not lost in those gray areas: gaining skill and increased self-control* . . . Ainslie, *Breakdown of Will*, 104.

101 *It is easier to avoid temptation than to overcome it* . . . Baumeister and Heatherton, "Self-Regulation Failure," 4.

103 *In experiments, dieters who feel they have* . . . C. P. Herman and J. Polivy, "Dieting as an Exercise in Behavioral Economics," in *Time and Decision: Economic and Psychological Perspectives on Intertemporal Choice*, edited by George Loewenstein, Daniel Read, and Roy F. Baumeister (New York: Russell Sage Foundation, 2003), 467.

103 *Being angry, tired, or lonely can make us* . . . Herman and Polivy, "Dieting as an Exercise in Behavioral Economics," 461–62.

5. Procrastination and Stress

110 *Studies from the 1970s* . . . A. Ellis, and W. J. Knaus, *Overcoming Procrastination* (New York: Institute for Rational Living, 1977).

110 *And according to 43Things.com* . . . http://www.43things.com/zeitgeistpopular_goals.

111 *But all hope is not lost* . . . Ranjita Misra and Michelle McKean, "College Students' Academic Stress and Its Relations to Their Anxiety, Time Management, and Leisure Satisfaction," *American Journal of Health Studies* 16, no. 1 (2000).

112 *People who put an assignment in their planner* . . . Norman A. Milgram, Barry Sroloff, and Michael Rosenbaum, "The Procrastination of Everyday Life," *Journal of Research in Personality* 22 (1988): 207.

113 *And if you're in a learning environment* . . . Dianne M. Tice and Roy F. Baumeister, "Longitudinal Study of Procrastination, Performance, Stress and Health: The Costs and Benefits of Dawdling," *Psychological Science* 8, no. 6 (November 1997).

113 *In study after study, researchers find that procrastinators* . . . Tice and Baumeister, "Longitudinal Study."

113 *And that leads to more stress* . . . Tice and Baumeister, "Longitudinal Study."

113 *Studies show that overoptimistic belief that you won't procrastinate* . . . T. O'Donoghue and M. Rabin, "Self-Awareness and Self-Control," in *Time and Decision*, ed. Loewenstein, Read, and Baumeister, 224.

114 *But this is a fatalistic attitude* . . . David Jacobson, "The Danger in Delay: Combat Procrastination," online at MedicineNet.com: http://www.medicinenet.com/script/main/art.asp?articlekey=50853.

114 *And while there are many reasons why people procrastinate* . . . Milgram, Sroloff, and Rosenbaum, "Procrastination of Everyday Life," 200.

115 *This can be a real issue* . . . Milgram, Sroloff, and Rosenbaum, "Procrastination of Everyday Life," 207.

117 *"Self-help is at the root of all genuine growth* . . . Samuel Smiles, *Self-Help*, ed. Ralph Lytton Bower (New York: American Book Co., 1904), 7.

118 *"each person's capacity for self-regulation* . . . Baumeister and Heatherton, "Self-Regulation Failure," 3.

120 *Research supports this idea* . . . Barbara A. Fritzsche, Beth Rapp Young, and Kara C. Hickson, "Individual Differences in Academic Procrastination Tendency and Writing Success," *Personality and Individual Differences* 35, no. 7 (November 2003): 1549–57.

121 *Do you eat the frosting first* . . . M. S. Peck, *The Road Less Traveled: A New Psychology of Love, Traditional Values and Spiritual Growth* (New York: Simon & Schuster, 1978), 19.

122 *Positive affirmations can replenish self-control* . . . B. J. Schmeichel and K. Vohs, "Self-Affirmation and Self-Control: Affirming Core Values Counteracts Ego Depletion," *Journal of Personal Social Psychology* 96, no. 4 (April 2009): 770–82 (article describing the study online at: http://www.spring.org.uk/2010/03/self-control-instantly-replenished-by-self-affirmation.php).

122 *And forgiving yourself for procrastination* . . . M. J. A. Wohl, T. A. Pychyl, and S. H.

Bennet, "I Forgive Myself, Now I Can Study: How Self-Forgiveness for Procrastinating Can Reduce Future Procrastination," *Personality and Individual Differences* (in press).

123 *It turns out that those who forgave themselves* . . . Wohl, Pychyl, and Bennet, "I Forgive Myself, Now I Can Study."

125 *But once we break through* . . . Stephen Covey, *The 7 Habits of Highly Effective People*, (1989; repr., New York: Fireside, 1990 edition), 46–47.

6. Thrift

135 *On the next page is one of the most popular psychological scales* . . . There's an online version of this at McGraw Hill, too http://highered.mcgraw-hill.com/sites/dl/free/0073531898/161461/chap16.swf.

138 *Then things changed, dramatically* . . . Robin Wilson, "A Lifetime of Student Debt?" *Chronicle of Higher Education*, May 22, 2009. See also "We Try Hard. We Fall Short. Americans Assess Their Saving Habits," Pew Report on Social and Demographic Trends, January 24, 2007, http://pewsocialtrends.org/pubs/325/we-try-hard-we-fall-short-americans-assess-their-saving-habits.

138 *Indeed, the United States saves less than* . . . Bankrate.com.

140 *Franklin wrote about thrift as industry* . . . Benjamin Franklin quotes are all over the web: http://www.quotationspage.com/quotes/Benjamin_Franklin/.

144 *In his book,* Whatever Happened to Thrift . . . Ronald Wilcox, *Whatever Happened to Thrift: Why Americans Don't Save and What to Do about It* (New Haven: Yale University Press, 2008), 3.

147 *Buying one thing—even one small thing* . . . Ravi Dhar, Joel Huber, and Uzma Khan, "The Shopping Momentum Effect," *Journal of Marketing Research* (August 2007). Also see article discussing this research at: http://www.gsb.stanford.edu/news/research/khan_shopping.html.

147 *But psychologists urge you to think about money globally* . . . For more information on these ideas, see Dan Ariely's book, *Predictably Irrational: The Hidden Forces That Shape Our Decisions* (New York: HarperCollins, 2008). Also see this short article: http://www.spring.org.uk/2008/04/avoid-relativity-trap-how-thinking.php.

147 *Research finds that emotional spending doesn't* . . . Jennifer Lerner, PhD, director of the Emotion and Decision Making Lab at Carnegie Mellon University research. C. E. Cryder, J. S. Lerner, J. J. Gross, and R. E. Dahl, "Misery Is Not Miserly: Sad and Self-Focused Individuals Spend More," *Psychological Science* 19 (2008): 525–30. And http://content.ksg.harvard.edu/lernerlab/media/6_common_shopping_traps.php.

147 *To get on track, people in their twenties and thirties* . . . Steve Hamm, "The New Age of Frugality," *Business Week*, October 20, 2008, http://www.businessweek.com/magazine/content/08_42/b4104054847273.htm.

153 *"When you understand what's important to you* . . . David Bach, *The Finish Rich Workbook* (New York: Broadway Books, 2003), 29.

157 *Bach guides readers through worksheets* . . . Bach, *Finish Rich Workbook*, 49.

165 *In his bestselling Finish Rich series* . . . Bach, *Finish Rich Workbook*, xiii.

165 *"Change your actions, change your life* . . . Bach, *Finish Rich Workbook*, xii, 11, 27, 28.

168 *Among the top tips* . . . Sandra Block, "In-Debt Grads with No Jobs Can Sidestep Student Loan Trouble," Your Money column, *USA Today*, May 25, 2010, http://www.usatoday.com/money/perfi/columnist/block/2010-05-25-yourmoney25_ST_N.htm.

169 *A life of drudgery and painfully working a job you don't like* . . . Suze Orman, *The Money Book for the Young, Fabulous, and Broke* (New York: Riverhead, 2005), 69.

176 *And, according to a retailer's study* . . . *Real Simple*, June 2010, 190.

176 *There's evidence that we feel richer when* . . . J. Quoidbach, E. W. Dunn, K. V. Petrides, and M. Mikolajczak, "Money Giveth, Money Taketh Away: The Dual Effect of Wealth on Happiness," *Psychological Science* (in press). See also L. Anik, L. B. Aknin, M. I. Norton, and E. W. Dunn, "Feeling Good about Giving: The Benefits (and Costs) of Self-Interested Charitable Behavior," in *Experimental Approaches to the Study of Charitable Giving*, ed. D. M. Oppenheimer and C. Y. Olivola (in press).

177 *Study after study seems to show* . . . Arthur C. Brooks, "Does Giving Make You Prosperous?" *Journal of Economics and Finance* 31, no. 3 (September 2007), http://www.springerlink.com/content/771347h671384k55/.

178 *"Each of our memories is different* . . . Suze Orman, *The 9 Steps to Financial Freedom* (New York: Three Rivers Press, 1997), 19.

180 *Welcome to the experience economy* . . . B. Joseph Pine II and James H. Gilmore, "Welcome to the Experience Economy," *Harvard Business Review* (July-August, 1998), 97–105. http://hbr.org/1998/07/welcome-to-the-experience-economy/ar/1.

180 *Six reasons* . . . Travis J. Carter and Thomas Gilovich, "The Relative Relativity of Material and Experiential Purchases," *Journal of Personality and Social Psychology* 98, no. 1 (January 2010): 146–59.

7. Become a Fearless You

184 *A smile is the universal language of welcome* . . . Carroll E. Izard, *The Face of Emotion* (New York: Appleton-Century-Croft, 1971).

184 *"Act as if you were already happy* . . . Dale Carnegie, *How to Win Friends and Influence People* (1936; repr., New York: Simon & Schuster, 1964), 99.

184 *Yes, we smile when we're happy* . . . J. D. Laird, *Feelings: The Perception of Self* (New York: Oxford University Press, 2007).

185 *A team of researchers at the University of Portsmouth* . . . Amy Drahota, Alan Costall, and Vasudevi Reddy, "The Vocal Communication of Different Kinds of Smile," *Speech Communication* 50, no. 4 (April 2008): 278–87.

186 *"If you are wrong, admit it quickly* . . . Carnegie, *How to Win Friends*, 164.

187 *'breaking lances with him* . . . Carnegie, *How to Win Friends*, 164.

188 *But it was Stephen Covey's advice* . . . Stephen Covey, *The 7 Habits of Highly Effective People* (1989; repr., New York: Fireside, 1990 edition), 219.

190 *To be an effective person means looking* . . . Covey, *The 7 Habits of Highly Effective People*, 234.

193 *"He that has once done you a kindness* . . . Richard Wiseman, *59 Seconds: Think a Little, Change a Lot* (New York: Knopf, 2009), 51–55.

195 *To achieve these goals* . . . Carnegie, *How to Win Friends and Influence People* (1936; repr., New York: Simon & Schuster, 1981), 25.

196 *"Let's remember that next time we* . . . Carnegie, *How to Win Friends and Influence People*, 89.

196 *"confirmed as much as it stimulated broad feelings* . . . D. Meyer, *The Positive Thinkers: Popular Religious Psychology from Mary Baker Eddy to Norman Vincent Peale and Ronald Reagan,* rev. sub. ed. (Middletown, CT: Wesleyan, 1988), 180.

199 *six principles for making people like you* . . . Carnegie, *How to Win Friends and Influence People*, 142.

200 *It's not luck that's going to get you that promotion* . . . Sharalyn Hartwell, "Generation Y believes in hard work to get ahead," *Philadelphia Examiner*, January 25, 2010, http://www.examiner.com/x-13207-Generation-Y-Examiner~y2010m1d25-Generation-Y-believes-in-hard-work-to-get-ahead.

203 *Out-of-Date Language, Totally Current Advice* . . . Samuel Smiles, *Duty* (London, 1880), 29, 33, 59–62.

8. Make Meaning

210 *Based on the results of the narcissistic personality inventory* . . . Jean Twenge and Joshua Foster, "Birth Cohort Increases in Narcissistic Personality Traits Among American College Students, 1982–2009," *Social Psychological and Personality Science* 1, no. 1 (2010): 99–106. Abstract at: http://spp.sagepub.com/cgi/content/abstract/1/1/99.

211 *According to Generation WTF surveys* . . . http://surveyu.com/ survey and PowerPoint available by request from author.

212 *"If you want others to like you* . . . Dale Carnegie, *How to Win Friends and Influence People* (1936; repr., New York: Simon & Schuster, 1981), 93–94.

214 *It's a weird quirk of our psychology* . . . John J. Skowronski, Donal E. Carlston, Lynda Mae, and Matthew T. Crawford, "Spontaneous Trait Transference: Communicators Take on the Qualities They Describe in Others," *Journal of Personality and Social Psychology* 74, no. 4 (1998).

214 *In his book* 59 Seconds . . . Richard Wiseman, *59 Seconds: Think a Little, Change a Lot* (New York: Knopf, 2009), 56.

215 *Some seventy-five years earlier* . . . Carnegie, *How to Win Friends*, 46.

216 *In* The 7 Habits of Highly Effective People . . . Stephen Covey, *The 7 Habits of Highly Effective People* (1989; repr., New York: Fireside, 1990 edition), 239.

218 *"College kids today are about 40 percent lower* . . . "Empathy: College students don't have as much as they used to," University of Michigan News Service, May 27, 2010, University of Michigan news service, available at http://www.ns.umich.edu/htdocs/releases/story.php?id=7724.

220 *Want to test yourself* . . . To take the survey off of the University of Michigan website it's here: http://umichisr.qualtrics.com/SE/?SID=SV_bCvraMmZBCcov52&SVI.

225 *The most common places to meet a match* . . . The Pew Internet and American Life 2006 report on "Romance in America," which can be found at: http://www.pewinternet.org/Reports/2006/Romance-in-America.aspx?r=1.

228 *This little puzzle was put together* . . . Shankar Vedantam, "Hidden Brain Puzzle Finding Love: Quantity vs Quality . . . Romance Depends on Quality, Not Quantity," *Psychology Today* blog, April 20, 2010, http://www.psychologytoday.com/blog/the-hidden-brain/201004/hidden-brain-puzzle-finding-love-quantity-vs-quality.

230 *Here's the problem: Research clearly shows* . . . Research from Daniel Lichter. For more on his work, see: http://www.soc.cornell.edu/faculty/lichter.html.

231 *According to research by University of Michigan sociologist* . . . Pamela Smock et al., "Heterosexual Cohabitation in the United States: Motives for Living Together among Young Men and Women," August 2006 report for the Population Studies Research Center. PDF download: http://www.psc.isr.umich.edu/pubs/pdf/rr06-606.pdf.

233 *Nick recalled a vignette* . . . Carnegie, *How to Win Friends and Influence People*, 16.

235 *Perhaps the more cynical among you* . . . Andrea Stone, "'Civic Generation' Rolls Up Sleeves in Record Numbers," *USA Today*, April 19. 2009, http://www.usatoday.com/news/sharing/2009-04-13-millenial_N.htm.

235 *Even if you don't feel like community service* . . . Research from Sonja Lyubomirsky, a professor of psychology at the University of California–Riverside. For more on this and other research by Professor Lyubomirsky, visit: http://www.faculty.ucr.edu/~sonja/.

237 *Generosity makes you feel good* . . . Suze Orman, *The 9 Steps to Financial Freedom* (New York: Three Rivers Press, 1997), 305.

239 *The message is clear* . . . Orman, *The 9 Steps to Financial Freedom*, 305.

Resources

WTF Do I Learn More?

Want more information? Here are some extra resources that might be of interest—chapter by chapter:

Chapter 1: Who Are You?

David Bach, *The Finish Rich Workbook* (New York: Broadway Books, 2003)

Richard N. Bolles, *What Color Is Your Parachute? 2010: A Practical Manual for Job-Hunters and Career-Changers* (New York: Ten Speed Press, 2009)

Stephen Covey, *The 7 Habits of Highly Effective People* (New York: Fireside, 1989)

William Damon, *The Path to Purpose* (New York: Free Press, 2008)

Nicholas Lore, *Now What?: The Young Person's Guide to Choosing the Perfect Career* (New York: Fireside, 2008)

M. Scott Peck, *The Road Less Traveled, 25th Anniversary Edition: A New Psychology of Love, Traditional Values and Spiritual Growth* (New York: Touchstone, 2003)

Chapter 2: Get Honest with Yourself

Phil McGraw, *Life Strategies* (New York: Hyperion, 1999)

Suze Orman, *The 9 Steps to Financial Freedom* (New York: Three Rivers Press, 1997)

Christopher Peterson and Martin Seligman, *Character Strengths and Virtues: A Handbook and Classification* (New York: Oxford University Press, 2004)

Laura Vanderkam, *168 Hours: You Have More Time Than You Think* (New York: Portfolio, 2010)

Richard Wiseman, *59 Seconds: Think a Little, Change a Lot* (New York: Knopf, 2009)

Chapter 3: Got Goal?

A. Bandura, *Self-Efficacy: The Exercise of Control* (New York: Worth Publishers, 1997)

Kenneth Blanchard and Spencer Johnson, *The One-Minute Manager* (New York: Berkley Trade, 1983)

Stephen Covey, *The 7 Habits of Highly Effective People* (New York: Fireside, 1989)

Daniel Coyle, *The Talent Code: Greatness Isn't Born. It's Grown. Here's How* (New York: Bantam, 2009)

M. Scott Peck, *The Road Less Traveled, 25th Anniversary Edition: A New Psychology of Love, Traditional Values and Spiritual Growth* (New York: Touchstone, 2003)

Richard Wiseman, *59 Seconds: Think a Little, Change a Lot* (New York: Knopf, 2009)

Chapter 4: Self-Control

Jonah Lehrer, "Don't," *New Yorker*, May 18, 2009.

Phil McGraw, *Life Strategies* (New York: Hyperion, 1999)

M. Scott Peck, *The Road Less Traveled, 25th Anniversary Edition: A New Psychology of Love, Traditional Values and Spiritual Growth* (New York: Touchstone, 2003)

A. Robbins, *Awaken the Giant Within: How to Take Immediate Control of*

Your Mental, Emotional, Physical and Financial Destiny (New York: Free Press, 1991)

Chapter 5: Procrastination and Stress

M. Scott Peck, *The Road Less Traveled, 25th Anniversary Edition: A New Psychology of Love, Traditional Values and Spiritual Growth* (New York: Touchstone, 2003)

The Procrastination Research Group in Ottawa, Canada, has a fun website with research, cartoons and many other links: http://http-server.carleton.ca/~tpychyl/

Samuel Smiles, *Self Help* (Available for free download at: http://www.gutenberg.org/etext/935)

Chapter 6: Thrift

Dan Ariely, *Predictably Irrational: The Hidden Forces That Shape Our Decisions* (New York: Harper Collins, 2008)

David Bach, *The Finish Rich Workbook* (New York: Broadway Books, 2003). Also online at http://www.finishrich.com

Amy Dacyczyn, *The Complete Tightwad Gazette* (New York: Villard, 1998)

Guy Kiyosaki, *Rich Dad, Poor Dad* (New York: Sphere, 2002)

Suze Orman, *The Money Book for the Young, Fabulous and Broke* (New York: Riverhead Hardcover, 2005). Plus, visit http://www.suzeorman.com for online Action Plan guides that correspond with *The Money Book* specifically geared toward Generation WTF needs.

Suze Orman, *The 9 Steps to Financial Freedom* (New York: Three Rivers Press, 1997)

Barty Phillips, *Thrifty Living* (New York: McGraw-Hill, 2010)

Dave Ramsey, *The Total Money Makeover* (Nashville: Thomas Nelson, 2009)

Samuel Smiles, *Thrift* (Available for free online here: http://www.gutenberg.org/etext/14418)

Ronald Wilcox, *Whatever Happened to Thrift: Why Americans Don't Save and What to Do about It* (New Haven: Yale University Press, 2008)

Chapter 7: Become a Fearless You

Dale Carnegie, *How to Win Friends and Influence People* (New York: Simon & Schuster, 1936)

Stephen Covey, *The 7 Habits of Highly Effective People* (New York: Fireside, 1989)

Samuel Smiles, *Duty* (London, 1880—available for free from GoogleReader and through many modern publishers reissuing his work)

Richard H. Thaler and Cass R. Sunstein, *Nudge: Improving Decisions About Health, Wealth, and Happiness* (New Haven: Yale University Press, 2008)

Chapter 8: Make Meaning

Dale Carnegie, *How to Win Friends and Influence People* (New York: Simon & Schuster, 1936)

Stephen Covey, *The 7 Habits of Highly Effective People* (New York: Fireside, 1989)

Dacher Keltner, *Born to Be Good: The Science of a Meaningful Life* (New York, W.W. Norton, 2009)

Sonja Lyubomirsky, *The How of Happiness: A New Approach to Getting the Life You Want* (New York: Penguin, 2008)

Suze Orman, *The 9 Steps to Financial Freedom* (New York: Three Rivers Press, 1997)

Shankar Vedantam, *The Hidden Brain: How Our Unconscious Minds Elect Presidents, Control Markets, Wage Wars, and Save Our Lives* (New York: Spiegel & Grau, 2010)

Richard Wiseman, *59 Seconds: Think a Little, Change a Lot* (New York: Knopf, 2009)